PRACTICAL COOKERY.

1. *Observations respecting Meat.*

MEAT to be in perfection should be kept a number of days when the weather will admit of it. Beef and mutton should be kept at least a week in cold weather, and poultry three or four days. If the weather is hot, it will keep but a short time. It should be kept in a cool, airy place, away from the flies, and if there is any danger of its spoiling, a little salt should be rubbed over it. When meat is frozen, it should be put into lukewarm water, and not taken out till the frost is extracted. If there is any frost in it when put to the fire, it will not cook well. The best way to boil it is to put it in cold water, and boil it gently, with just water enough to cover it, as it hardens by furious boiling. The part that is to be up on the table, should be down in the pot, as the scum that rises is apt to make the meat look dark—the scum should be taken off as soon as it rises. The liquor in which all kinds of fresh meat is boiled, makes a good soup, when thickened and seasoned. Boiling is the cheapest way of cooking meat, provided you make a soup of the liquor; if not, it is the dearest, as most of the gelatine is extracted by the process of boiling, which is the most nourishing part, and if not used for soup, is completely lost. In roasting meat, only the juices and fat are extracted, but not lost, as the juices make good gravy, and the fat is good for various culinary purposes. When it is put down to roast, there should be a little water in the dripping pan. For broiling, the bars of the gridiron should be perfectly clean, and greased with lard or butter, otherwise the meat will retain the impression of the bars. The bars of the gridiron should be concave, and terminate in a trough, to catch the juices, or they will drop in the fire and smoke the meat. A good fire of hot coals is necessary to have the meat broil as quick as possible without burning. The gridiron should be put on the fire, and well heated before the meat is laid on it. The dish should be very hot on which broiled meat is put, and it should not be seasoned till taken up. If you wish to fry meat, cut a small piece of pork into slices, and fry them a light brown, then take them up and put in your meat, which should be perfectly dry. When the meat is sufficiently fried, take it up, remove the frying pan from the fire to cool; when so, turn in a little cold water for the gravy, put it on the fire—when it boils, stir in a little mixed flour and water, let it boil, then turn it over the meat. If not rich enough, add butter and catsup if you like.

2. *Roast Beef.*

The tender loin and first and second cuts off the rack are the best roasting pieces—the third and fourth cuts are good. When the meat is put to the fire, a little salt should be sprinkled on it, and the bony side turned towards the fire first. When the bones get well heated through, turn the meat, and keep a brisk fire—baste it frequently while roasting. There should be a little water put into the dripping pan when the meat is put down to roast. If it is a thick piece, allow fifteen minutes to each pound to roast it in—if thin, less time will be required.

3. *Beef Steak.*

The tender loin is the best piece for broiling—a steak from the round or shoulder clod is good and comes cheaper. If the beef is not very tender, it should be laid on a board and pounded, before broiling or frying it. Wash it in cold water, then lay it on a gridiron, place it on a hot bed of coals, and broil it as quick as possible without burning it. If broiled slow, it will not be good. It takes from fifteen to twenty minutes to broil a steak. For seven or eight pounds of beef, cut up about a quarter of a pound of butter. Heat the platter very hot that the steak is to be put on, lay the butter on it, take up the steak, salt and pepper it on both sides. Beef steak to be good, should be eaten as soon as cooked. A few slices of salt pork broiled with the steak makes a rich gravy with a very little butter. There should always be a trough to catch the juices of the meat when broiled. The same pieces that are good broiled are good for frying. Fry a few slices of salt pork, brown, then take them up and put in the beef. When brown on both sides, take it up, take the pan off from the fire, to let the fat cool; when cool, turn in half a tea cup of water, mix a couple of tea spoonsful of flour with a little water, stir it into the fat, put the pan back on the fire, stir it till it boils up, then turn it over the beef.

4. *Alamode Beef.*

The round of beef is the best piece to alamode—the shoulder clod is good, and comes lower; it is also good stewed, without any spices. For five pounds of beef, soak about a pound of bread in cold water till soft, then drain off the water, mash the bread fine, put in a piece of butter, of the size of a hen's egg, half a tea spoonful of salt, the same quantity of ground cloves, allspice, and pepper, half a nutmeg, a couple of eggs, and a table spoonful of flour—mix the whole well together; then cut gashes in the beef, and fill them with about half of the dressing, put the meat in a bake-pan, with lukewarm water enough to cover it; set it where it will stew gently for a couple of hours, cover it with a heated bake pan lid. When it has stewed a couple of hours, turn the reserved dressing on top of the meat, heat the bake pan lid hot enough to brown the dressing, stew it an hour and a half longer. After the meat is taken up, if the gravy is not thick enough, mix a tea spoonful or two of flour with a little water, and stir it into the gravy; put in a little butter, a wine glass of wine, and turn it over the meat.

5. *Beef Liver.*

Liver is very good fried, but the best way to cook it, is to broil it ten minutes, with four or five slices of salt pork. Then take it, cut it into small strips together with the pork, put it in a stew pan, with a little water, butter, and pepper. Stew it four or five minutes.

6. *To Corn Beef.*

To every gallon of cold water, put a quart of rock salt, an ounce of salt-petre, quarter of a pound of brown sugar—(some people use molasses, but it is not as good)—no boiling is necessary. Put the beef in the brine. As long as any salt remains at the bottom of the cask it is strong enough. Whenever any scum rises, the brine should be scalded, skimmed, and more sugar, salt and salt-petre added. When a piece of beef is put in the brine, rub a little salt over it. If the weather is hot, cut a gash to the bone of the meat, and fill it with salt. Put a heavy weight on the beef in order to keep it under the brine. In very hot weather, it is difficult to corn beef in cold brine before it spoils. On this account it is good to corn it in the pot when boiled. It is done in the following manner; to six or eight pounds of beef, put a tea cup of salt, sprinkle flour on the side that is to go up on the table, and put it down in the pot, turn the water into the pot after the beef is put in, boil it a couple of hours, then turn in more cold water, and boil it an hour and a half longer.

7. *Mutton.*

The saddle is the best part to roast—the shoulder and leg are good roasted; but the best mode to cook the latter, is to boil it with a piece of salt pork. A little rice boiled with it, improves the looks of it. Mutton for roasting, should have a little butter rubbed on it, and a little salt and pepper sprinkled on it—some people like cloves and allspice. Put a small piece of butter in the dripping pan, and baste it frequently. The bony side should be turned towards the fire first, and roasted. For boiling or roasting mutton, allow a quarter of an hour to each pound of meat. The leg is good cut in gashes, and filled with a dressing, and baked. The dressing is made of soaked bread, a little butter, salt, and pepper, and a couple of eggs. A pint of water with a little butter should be put in the pan. The leg is also good, cut into slices and broiled. It is good corned a few days, and then boiled. The rack is good for broiling—it should be divided, each bone by itself, broiled quick, and buttered, salted and peppered. The breast of mutton is nice baked. The joints of the brisket should be separated, the sharp ends of the ribs sawed off, the outside rubbed over with a little piece of butter—salt it, and put it in a bake pan, with a pint of water. When done, take it up, and thicken the gravy with a little flour and water, and put in a small piece of butter. A table spoonful of catsup, cloves and allspice, improve it, but are not essential. The neck of mutton makes a good soup. Parsely or celery-heads are a pretty garnish for mutton.

8. *Veal.*

The loin of veal is the best piece for roasting. The breast and rack are good roasted. The breast also is good made into a pot pie, and the rack cut into small pieces and broiled. The leg is nice for frying, and when several slices have been cut off for cutlets, the remainder is nice boiled with a small piece of salt pork. Veal for roasting should be salted, peppered, and a little butter rubbed on it, and basted frequently. Put a little water in the dripping pan, and unless the meat is quite fat, a little butter should be put in. The fillet is good baked, the bone should be cut out, and the place filled with a dressing, made of bread soaked soft in cold water, a little salt, pepper, a couple of eggs, and a table spoonful of melted butter put in—then sew it up, put it in your bake pan, with about a pint of water, cover the top of the meat with some of the dressing. When baked sufficiently, take it up, thicken the gravy with a little flour and water well mixed, put in a small piece of butter, and a little wine and catsup, if you like the gravy rich.

9. *Veal Cutlets.*

Fry three or four slices of pork until brown—take them up, then put in slices of veal, about an inch thick, cut from the leg. When brown on both sides, take them up—stir half a pint of water into the gravy, then mix two or three tea spoonsful of flour with a little water, and stir it in—soak a couple of slices of toasted bread in the gravy, lay them on the bottom of the platter, place the meat and pork over it, then turn on the gravy. A very nice way to cook the cutlets, is to make a batter with half a pint of milk, an egg beaten to a froth, and flour enough to render it thick. When the veal is fried brown, dip it into the batter, then put it back into the fat, and fry it until brown again. If you have any batter left, it is nice dropped by the large spoonful into the fat, and fried till brown, then laid over the veal. Thicken the gravy and turn it over the whole. It takes about an hour to cook this dish. If the meat is tough, it will be better to stew it half an hour before frying it.

10. *Calf's Head.*

Boil the head two hours, together with the lights and feet. Put in the liver when it has boiled an hour and twenty minutes. Before the head is done, tie the brains in a bag, and boil them with it; when the brains are done, take them up, season them with salt, pepper, butter, and sweet herbs, or spices if you like—use this as a dressing for the head. Some people prefer part of the liver and feet for dressing—they are prepared like the brains. The liquor that the calf's head is boiled in, makes a good soup, seasoned in a plain way like any other veal soup, or seasoned turtle fashion. The liquor should stand until the next day after the head is boiled, in order to have the fat rise, and skimmed off. If you wish to have your calf's head look brown, take it up when tender, rub a little butter over it, sprinkle on salt, pepper, and allspice—sprinkle flour over it, and put before the fire, with a Dutch oven over it, or in a brick oven where it will brown quick. Warm up the brains with a little water, butter, salt, and pepper. Add wine and spices if you like. Serve it up as a dressing for the head. Calf's head is also good, baked. Halve it, rub butter over it, put it in a pan, with about a quart of water; then cover it with a dressing made of bread soaked soft, a little butter, an egg, and season it with salt, pepper, and powdered mace. Slice up the brains, and lay them in the pan with the head. Bake it in a quick oven, and garnish it with slices of lemon, or force meat balls.

11. *Force Meat Balls.*

Chop a pound or two of veal fine—mix it with one or two eggs, a little butter, or raw pork chopped fine—season it with salt and pepper, or curry powder. Do them up into balls about the size of half an egg, and fry them brown.

12. *Calf's Feet.*

Boil them with the head, until tender, then split and lay them round the head, or dredge them with flour after they have been boiled tender, and fry them brown. If you wish for gravy for them, when you have taken them up, stir a little flour into the fat they were fried in; season it with salt, pepper, and mace. Add a little butter and wine if you like, then turn it over the feet.

13. *Calf's Liver and Heart.*

Are good, broiled or fried. Some people like the liver stuffed and baked.

14. *Collops.*

Cut part of a leg of veal into pieces, three or four inches broad—sprinkle flour on them, fry them in butter until brown, then turn in water enough to cover the veal. When it boils, take off the scum, put in two or three onions, a blade of mace, a little salt and pepper. When stewed tender, take up the meat, thicken the gravy with flour and water, mixed smoothly together, squeeze in the juice of half a lemon, then turn it over the collops. Garnish them with a lemon cut in thin slices.

15. *Plaw.*

Boil a piece of lean veal till tender. Take it up, cut it into strips three or four inches long, put it back into the pot, with the liquor it was boiled in, with a tea cup of rice to three pounds of veal. Put in a piece of butter, of the size of a hen's egg; season it with salt, pepper, and sweet herbs if you like; stew it gently till the rice is tender, and the water nearly stewed away. A little curry powder in this, converts it into a curry dish.

16. *A Fillet of Veal.*

Cut off the shank of a leg of veal, and cut gashes in the remainder. Make a dressing of bread, soaked soft in cold water, and mashed; season it with salt, pepper, and sweet herbs; chop a little raw pork fine, put it in the dressing, and if you have not pork, use a little butter instead. Fill the gashes in the meat with part of the dressing, put it in a bake pan, with just water enough to cover it; put the remainder of the dressing on top of the meat, and cover it with a heated bake pan lid. For six pounds of veal, allow two hours' steady baking. A leg of veal is nice prepared in this manner, and roasted.

17. *Lamb.*

The fore and hind quarters are good roasting pieces. Sprinkle salt and pepper on the lamb, turn the bony side towards the fire first; if not fat, rub a little butter on it, and put a little in the dripping pan; baste it frequently. These pieces are good stuffed like a fillet of veal, and roasted. The leg is also good, cooked in the same manner; but it is better boiled with a pound of salt pork. Allow fifteen minutes boiling to each pound of meat. The breast of lamb is good roasted, broiled, or corned and boiled; it is also good made into a pot pie. The fore quarter, with the ribs divided, is good broiled. The bones of this, as well as all kinds of meat, when put down to broil, should first be put towards the fire, and browned before the other side is broiled. A little salt, pepper, and butter, should be put on it when you take it up. Lamb is very apt to spoil in warm weather. If you wish to keep a leg several days, put it in brine. It should not be put with pork, as fresh meat is apt to injure it. Lamb's head, feet, and heart, are good, boiled till tender, then cut off the flesh from the head, cut up the heart, and split the feet in two; put the whole into a pan, with a pint of the liquor they were boiled in, together with a little butter, pepper, salt, and half a tea cup of tomato catsup; thicken the gravy with a little flour; stew the whole for a few moments. Pepper-grass, or parsely, are a pretty garnish for this dish.

18. *Shoulder of Lamb Grilled.*

The shoulder of lamb is good roasted plain, but is better cooked in the following manner. Score it in checkers, about an inch long, rub it over with a little butter, and the yelk of an egg; then dip it into finely pounded bread crumbs; sprinkle on salt, pepper, and sweet herbs; roast it till of a light brown. This is good with plain gravy, but better with a sauce, made in the following manner. Take a quarter of a pint of the drippings from the meat, mix it with the same quantity of water, set it on the fire; when it boils up, thicken it with a little flour and water mixed, put in a table spoonful of tomato catsup, the juice and grated rind of a lemon; season it with salt and pepper.

19. *Lamb's Fry.*

The heart and sweet bread are nice fried plainly, or dipped into a beaten egg and fine bread crumbs. They should be fried in lard.

20. *Turkey.*

Take out the inwards, wash both the inside and outside of the turkey. Prepare a dressing made of bread, soaked soft in cold water, (the water should be drained from the bread, and the bread mashed fine.) Melt a small piece of butter, and mix it with the dressing, or else put in salt pork, chopped fine; season it with salt and pepper; add sweet herbs if you like. An egg in the dressing, makes it cut smoother. Any kind of cooked meat is nice minced fine, and mixed with the dressing. If the inwards are used, they ought to be boiled very tender, as it is very difficult to cook them through while the turkey is roasting. Fill the crop and body of the turkey with the dressing, sew it up, tie up the legs and wings, rub on a little salt and butter. Roast it from two to three hours, according to its size; twenty-five minutes to every pound, is a good rule. The turkey should be roasted slowly at first, and basted frequently. A little water should be put into the dripping pan, when the meat is put down to roast. For a gravy to the turkey, take the liquor that the inwards are boiled in, put into it a little of the turkey drippings, set it where it will boil, thicken it with a little flour and water, previously mixed smooth. Season it with salt, pepper, and sweet herbs if you like. Drawn butter is used for boiled turkey. A turkey for boiling should be prepared in the same manner as one for roasting. If you wish to have it look white, tie it up in a cloth, unless you boil rice in the pot. If rice is used, put in two-thirds of a tea cup. A pound or two of salt pork, boiled with the turkey, improves it. If you wish to make a soup of the liquor in which the turkey is boiled, let it remain until the next day, then skim off the fat. Heat and season it.

21. *Goose.*

If a goose is tender under the wing, and you can break the skin easily by running the head of a pin across the breast, there is no danger of its being tough. A goose should be dressed in the same manner, and roasted the same length of time as a turkey.

22. *Chickens.*

Chickens for roasting or boiling should have a dressing prepared like that for turkies. Half a tea cup of rice boiled with the chickens makes them look white. They will be less liable to break if the water is cold when they are put in. A little salt pork boiled with the chickens, improves them. If you do not boil pork with them they will need salt. Chickens for broiling should be split, the inwards taken out, and the chicken washed inside and out. Put the bony side down on the gridiron, and broil it very slowly until brown, then turn it, and brown it on the other side. About forty minutes is required to broil a common sized chicken. For roast chicken, boil the liver and gizzards by themselves, and use the water for gravy to the chickens—cut the inwards in slices, and put them in the gravy.

23. *Fricassee.*

The chickens should be jointed, the inwards taken out, and the chickens washed. Put them in a stew pan with the skin side down; on each layer sprinkle salt and pepper; put in three or four slices of pork, just cover them with water, and let them stew till tender. Then take them up, mix a little flour and water together, and thicken the liquor they were stewed in, add a piece of butter of the size of a hen's egg, then put the chickens back in the stew pan, and let them stew four or five minutes longer. When you have taken up the chickens, soak two or three slices of toast in the gravy, then put them in your platter, lay the chickens over the toast, and turn the gravy on them. If you wish to brown the chickens, stew them without the pork, till tender, then fry the pork brown, take it up, put in the chickens, and then fry until a light brown.

24. *Pigeons.*

Take out the inwards, and stuff the pigeons with a dressing prepared like that for turkeys, lay them in a pot with the breast side down. Turn in more than enough water to cover them. When stewed nearly tender, put in a quarter of a pound of butter to every dozen of pigeons—mix two or three tea spoonsful of flour, with a little water, and stir into the gravy. If you wish to brown them, put on a heated bake pan lid, an hour before they are done, or else take them up when tender, and fry them in pork fat. They are very good split open and stewed, with a dressing made and warmed up separately with a little of the gravy. Tender pigeons are good stuffed and roasted. It takes about two hours to cook tender pigeons, and three hours tough ones. Roast pigeons should be buttered when put to the fire.

25. *Ducks.*

Are good stewed like pigeons, or roasted. Two or three onions in the dressing of wild ducks, takes out the fishy taste they are apt to have. If ducks or any other fowls are slightly injured by being kept long, dip them in weak saleratus water before cooking them.

26. *Baked or Roast Pig.*

A pig for roasting or baking should be small and fat. Take out the inwards, and cut off the first joint of the feet, and boil them till tender, then chop them. Prepare a dressing of bread soaked soft, the water squeezed out, and the bread mashed fine, season it with salt, pepper, and sweet herbs, add a little butter, and fill the pig with the dressing. Rub a little butter on the outside of the pig, to prevent its blistering. Bake or roast it from two hours and a half, to three hours. The pan that the pig is baked in should have a little water put in it. When cooked, take out a little of the dressing and gravy from the pan, mix it with the chopped inwards and feet, put in a little butter, pepper, and salt, and use this for a sauce to the pig. Expose the pig to the open air two or three minutes, before it is put on the table, to make it crispy.

27. *Sweet Bread, Liver, and Heart.*

A very good way to cook the sweet bread, is to fry three or four slices of pork till brown, then take them up and put in the sweet bread, and fry it over a moderate fire. When you have taken up the sweet bread, mix a couple of tea-spoonsful of flour with a little water, and stir it into the fat—let it boil, then turn it over the sweet bread. Another way is to parboil them, and let them get cold, then cut them in pieces about an inch thick, dip them in the yelk of an egg, and fine bread crumbs, sprinkle salt, pepper, and sage on them, before dipping them in the egg, fry them a light brown. Make a gravy after you have taken them up, by stirring a little flour and water mixed smooth into the fat, add spices and wine if you like. The liver and heart are good cooked in the same manner, or broiled.

28. *Pressed Head.*

Pig's head is good baked with beans, or corned and smoked. It is also nice prepared with spices in the following manner. Boil the ears, forehead, and rind, (the cheek is good, but it is better corned and smoked,) till the meat will almost drop from the bones; take them up; when cold cut the meat in strips about an inch long, warm it in a little of the liquor in which the meat was boiled, season it with salt, pepper, cloves, nutmeg, and cinnamon. Put it while hot in a strong bag, put a heavy weight upon it, and let it remain till perfectly cold. When you wish to eat it, cut it in thin slices.

29. *Souse.*

Take pig's ears and feet, clean them thoroughly, then soak them in salt and water, for several days. Boil them tender, and split them, they are then good fried. If you wish to souse them when cold, turn boiling vinegar on them, spiced with pepper-corns, and mace. Cloves improve the taste, but it turns them a dark color. Add a little salt. They will keep good pickled five or six weeks. Fry them in lard.

30. *Tripe.*

After being scoured, should be soaked in salt and water seven or eight days, changing the water every other day, then boil it till tender, which will take eight or ten hours. It is then fit for broiling, frying, or pickling. It is pickled in the same manner as souse.

31. *Sausages.*

Chop fresh pork very fine, the lean and fat together, (there should be rather more of the lean than the fat,) season it highly with salt, pepper, sage, and other sweet herbs, if you like them—a little salt-petre tends to preserve them. To tell whether they are seasoned enough, do up a little into a cake, and fry it. If not seasoned enough, add more seasoning, and fill your skins, which should be previously cleaned thoroughly. A little flour mixed in with the meat, tends to prevent the fat from running out when cooked. Sausage-meat is good, done up in small cakes and fried. In summer, when fresh pork cannot be procured, very good sausage-cakes may be made of raw beef, chopped fine with salt pork, and seasoned with pepper and sage. When sausages are fried, they should not be pricked, and they will cook nicer, to have a little fat put in the frying-pan with them. They should be cooked slowly. If you do not like them very fat, take them out of the pan when nearly done, and finish cooking them on a gridiron. Bologna sausages are made of equal weight each, of ham, veal, and pork, chopped very fine, seasoned high, and boiled in casings, till tender, then dried.

32. *Ham.*

A ham that weighs ten pounds, should be boiled four or five hours; if very salt, the water should be changed. Before it is put on the table, take off the rind. If you wish to ornament it, put whole cloves, or pepper, in the form of diamonds, over it. The Virginia method of curing hams, (which is considered very superior), is to dissolve two ounces of salt-petre, two tea spoonsful of saleratus, in a salt pickle, as strong as possible, for every sixteen pounds of ham, add molasses in the proportion of a gallon to a hogshead of brine, then put in the hams, and let them remain three or four weeks. Then take them out of the brine, and smoke them with the hocks downwards, to preserve the juices. They will smoke tolerably well, in the course of a month, but they will be much better, to remain in the smoke-house two or three months. Hams cured in this manner are very fine flavored, and will keep good a long time.

33. *Tongues.*

Cut off the roots of the tongues, they are not good smoked, but they make nice pies. Take out the pipes and veins, boil them till tender, mince them fine, season the meat with salt, cloves, mace, and cinnamon, put in a little sugar and molasses, moisten the whole with brandy, put it in a cool place, and it will keep good several months in cold weather, and is good to make pies of at any time, with the addition of apples chopped fine, and a little butter melted. For the remainder of the tongues, make a brine in the following manner—to a gallon of cold water, put a quart of rock salt, an ounce of salt-petre, quarter of a pound of sugar, and a couple of table spoonsful of blown salt. Put in the tongues, let them remain in it a week, and then smoke them eight or ten days.

34. Curries.

Chickens, pigeons, mutton chops, lobsters and veal, all make good curries. If the curry dish is to be made of fowls, they should be jointed. Boil the meat till tender, in just sufficient water to cover it, and add a little salt. Just before the meat is boiled enough to take up, fry three or four slices of pork till brown—take them up, and put in the chickens. Let them brown, then add part of the liquor in which they were boiled, one or two tea spoonsful of curry powder, and the fried pork. Mix a tea spoonful of curry powder with a tea cup of boiled rice, or a little flour and water mixed—turn it on to the curry, and let it stew a few minutes.

35. Chicken Pie.

Joint the chickens, which should be young and tender—boil them in just sufficient water to cover them. When nearly tender, take them out of the liquor, and lay them in a deep pudding dish, lined with pie crust. To each layer of chicken, put three or four slices of pork—add a little of the liquor in which they were boiled, and a couple of ounces of butter, cut into small pieces—sprinkle a little flour over the whole, cover it with nice pie crust, and ornament the top with some of your pastry. Bake it in a quick oven one hour.

36. Beef and Mutton Pie.

Take tender meat, pound it out thin, and broil it ten minutes—then cut off the bony and gristly parts, season it highly with salt and pepper, butter it, and cut it into small pieces. Line a pudding dish with pastry, put in the meat, and to each layer add a tea spoonful of tomato catsup, together with a table spoonful of water—sprinkle over flour, and cover it with pie crust, and ornament as you please with pastry. Cold roast, or boiled beef, and mutton, make a good pie, by cutting them into bits, and seasoning them highly with salt and pepper. Put them into a pie dish, turn a little melted butter over them, or gravy, and pour in water till you can just see it at the top.

37. Chicken and Veal Pot Pie.

If the pie is to be made of chickens, joint them—boil the meat until about half done. Take the meat out of the liquor in which it was boiled, and put it in a pot, with a layer of crust to each layer of meat, having a layer of crust on the top. The meat should be seasoned with salt and pepper—cover the whole with the boiled meat liquor. If you wish to have the crust brown, keep the pot covered with a heated bake pan lid. Keep a tea kettle of boiling water to turn in as the water boils away—cold water makes the crust heavy. The crust for the pie is good like that made for fruit pies, with less shortening, but raised pie crust is generally preferred to any other. It is made in the following manner—mix together three pints of flour, a tea cup of melted butter, a tea spoonful of salt, then turn in half a tea cup of yeast—add cold water to make it sufficiently stiff to roll out. Set it in a warm place to rise, which will take seven or eight hours, unless brewer's yeast is used. When risen, roll it out, and cut it into small cakes. Potatoe pie crust is very nice. To make it, boil eight or nine small potatoes, peel and mash them fine, mix with them a piece of butter, of the size of a hen's egg, a tea spoonful of salt, a tumbler full of milk, and flour to render it of the right consistency to roll out. When rolled out, cut them into cakes, and put them with the meat. If you happen to have unbaked wheat dough, very good crust may be made of it, by working into it a little lukewarm melted butter. Let it remain, after you have rolled and cut it into cakes, about ten or fifteen minutes, before putting it with the meat.

38. *To Frizzle Beef.*

Take beef that is fresh smoked and tender—shave it off thin, put it in a stew pan, with water enough to cover it—let it stew ten or fifteen minutes. Three or four minutes before it is taken up, mix a little flour and water together, and stir in, to thicken the water; add a little butter and pepper. This makes a good dish for breakfast—eggs are a nice accompaniment to it.

39. *Warmed Over Meats.*

Boiled or roasted veal makes a nice dish, chopped fine, and warmed up, with just sufficient water to moisten it, and a little butter, salt, and pepper, added. A little nutmeg, and the grated rind of a lemon, improve it—none of the white part of the lemon should be used. When well heated through, take it up on a platter, and garnish it with a couple of lemons cut in slices. Fresh or corned beef is good minced fine, with boiled potatoes, and warmed up with salt, pepper, and a little water—add butter, just before you take it up. Some people use the gravy that they have left the day before, for the meat, but it is not as good when warmed over, and there is no need of its being wasted, as it can be clarified, and used for other purposes. Boiled onions, or turnips, are good mixed with mince meat, instead of potatoes. Veal, lamb, and mutton, are good cut into small strips, and warmed with boiled potatoes cut in slices, pepper, salt, a little water—add butter just before you take it up. Roast beef and mutton, if not previously cooked too much, are nice cut in slices, and just scorched on a gridiron. Meat, when warmed over, should be on the fire just long enough to get well heated through—if on the fire long, most of the juices of the meat will be extracted, and render it very indigestible. Cold fowls are nice jointed, and warmed with a little water, then taken up, and fried in butter till brown. A little flour should be sprinkled on them before frying. Thicken the water that the fowls were warmed in—add a little salt, pepper, and butter, and turn it over the fowls.

40. *A Ragout of Cold Veal.*

Cut boiled or roasted veal in nice slices—flour and fry them in butter, till a light brown—then take them up, and turn a little hot water into the butter they were fried in, mix a little flour and water together, and stir it into the gravy—season it with salt, pepper, (nutmeg, or catsup,) and lemon juice—put in the meat, and stew it till very hot—stew two or three onions with it, if you like.

41. *Drawn Butter.*

Mix two or three tea spoonsful of flour with a little cold water—stir it till free from lumps, thin it, and stir it into half a pint of boiling water—let it boil two or three minutes, then cut up about a quarter of a pound of butter into small pieces, and put it with the flour and water—set it where it will melt gradually. If carefully mixed, it will be free from lumps—if not, strain it before it is put on the table. If the butter is to be eaten on fish, cut up several soft boiled eggs into it. A little curry powder sprinkled into it, will convert it into curry sauce.

42. *Burnt Butter.*

Put a couple of ounces of butter into a frying pan—set it on the fire—when of a dark brown color, put in half a tea cup full of vinegar, a little pepper and salt. This is nice for fish, salad, or eggs.

43. *Roast Meat Gravy.*

Meat, when put down to roast, should have about a pint of water in the dripping pan. A little while before the meat is done, stir up the drippings, put it in a skillet, and set it where it will boil. Mix two or three tea spoonsful of flour smoothly, with a little water, and stir it in the gravy when it boils. Lamb and veal require a little butter in the gravy. The gravy for pork and geese, should have a little of the dressing, and sage, mixed with it. If you wish to have your gravies look dark, scorch the flour that you thicken them with, which is easily done by putting it in a pan, setting it on a few coals, and stirring it constantly till it is a dark brown color, taking care that it does not burn. Enough can be burnt at once to last a long time.

44. *Sauce for Cold Meat, Fish or Salad.*

Boil a couple of eggs three minutes—then mix it with a mustard spoonful of made mustard, a little salt, pepper, half a tea cup of salad oil, or melted butter, and half a tea cup of vinegar. A table spoonful of catsup improves it.

45. *Wine Sauce for Venison or Mutton.*

Warm half a pint of the drippings, or liquor the meat was boiled in—mix a couple of tea spoonsful of scorched flour with a little water, and stir it in when the gravy boils. Season it with salt, pepper, and cloves—stir a table spoonful of currant jelly in, and just before you take it from the fire, half a tumbler of wine. Many people prefer melted currant jelly to any other sauce for venison or mutton.

46. *Rice Sauce.*

Boil one onion and half a tea cup of rice with a blade of mace, till very soft, in just water enough to cover it—then stir in half a pint of milk, a little salt, and strain it. This is a nice accompaniment to game.

47. *Oyster Sauce.*

Take the juice of the oysters, and to a pint put a couple of sticks of mace, a little salt and pepper. Set it on the fire—when it boils, stir in a couple of tea spoonsful of flour, mixed with milk. When it has boiled several minutes, stir in half a pint of oysters, a piece of butter, of the size of a hen's egg. Let them scald through, then take them up.

48. *White Celery Sauce for Boiled Poultry.*

Take five or six heads of celery—cut off the green tops, cut up the remainder into small bits, and boil it till tender, in half a pint of water—mix two or three tea spoonsful of flour smoothly with a little milk—then add half a tea cup more of milk, stir it in, add a small lump of butter, and a little salt. When it boils, take it up.

49. *Brown Sauce for Poultry.*

Peel two or three onions, cut them in slices, flour and fry them brown, in a little butter—then sprinkle in a little flour, pepper, salt, and sage—add half a pint of the liquor the poultry was boiled in, and a table spoonful of catsup. Let it boil up, then stir in half a wine glass of wine if you like.

50. *Savory Jelly for Cold Meat.*

Boil lean beef or veal till tender. If you have any beef or veal bones, crack and boil them with the meat, (they should be boiled longer than the meat,) together with a little salt pork, sweet herbs, and pepper and salt. When boiled sufficiently, take it off, strain it, and let it remain till the next day—then skim off the fat, take up the jelly, and scrape off the dregs that adhere to the bottom of it—put in the whites and shells of several eggs, several blades of mace, a little wine, and lemon juice—set it on the fire, stir it well till it boils, then strain it till clear through a jelly bag.

51. *Liver Sauce for Fish.*

Boil the liver of the fish—then mash it fine, stir it into drawn butter, put in a little cayenne, or black pepper, a couple of tea spoonsful of lemon juice, and a table spoonful of catsup.

52. *Sauce for Lobsters.*

Boil a couple of eggs three minutes—mix them with the spawn of the lobster, and a tea spoonful of water. When rubbed smooth, stir in a tea spoonful of mixed mustard, half a tea cup of salad oil, or the same quantity of butter melted, a little salt, pepper, and five table spoonsful of vinegar.

53. *Chicken Salad.*

Boil a chicken that weighs not more than a pound and a half. When very tender, take it up, cut it in small strips, and make the following sauce, and turn over it—boil four eggs three minutes—then take them out of the shells, mash and mix them with a couple of table spoonsful of olive oil, or melted butter, two thirds of a tumbler of vinegar, a tea spoonful of mixed mustard, a tea spoonful of salt, a little pepper, and essence of celery, if you have it—if not, it can be dispensed with.

54. *Sauce for Turtle, or Calf's Head.*

To half a pint of hot melted butter, or beef gravy, put the juice and grated rind of half a lemon, a little sage, basil, or sweet marjoram, a little cayenne, or black pepper, and salt. Add a wine glass of white wine just before you take it up.

55. *Apple and Cranberry Sauce.*

Pare and quarter the apples—if not tart, stew them in cider—if tart enough, stew them in water. When stewed soft, put in a small piece of butter, and sweeten it to the taste, with sugar. Another way, which is very good, is to boil the apples, without paring them, with a few quinces and molasses, in new cider, till reduced to half the quantity. When cool, strain the sauce. This kind of sauce will keep good several months. It makes very good plain pies, with the addition of a little cinnamon or cloves. To make cranberry sauce, nothing more is necessary than to stew the cranberries till soft; then stir in sugar and molasses to sweeten it. Let the sugar scald in it a few minutes. Strain it if you like—it is very good without straining.

56. *Pudding Sauce.*

Stir to a cream a tea cup of butter, with two of brown sugar, then add a wine glass of wine, or cider—flavor it with nutmeg, rose-water, or essence of lemon. If you wish to have it liquid, heat two-thirds of a pint of water boiling hot, mix two or three tea spoonsful of flour with a little water, and stir it into the boiling water. As soon as its boils up well, stir it into the butter and sugar.

57. *Tomato Soy.*

Take ripe tomatos, and prick them with a fork—lay them in a deep dish, and to each layer put a layer of salt. Let them remain in it four or five days, then take them out of the salt, and put them in vinegar and water for one night. Drain off the vinegar, and to each peck of tomatos put half a pint of mustard seed, half an ounce of cloves, and the same quantity of pepper. The tomatos should be put in a jar, with a layer of sliced onions to each layer of the tomatos, and the spices sprinkled over each layer. In ten days, they will be in good eating order.

58. *Tomato Catsup.*

To a gallon of ripe tomatos, put four table spoonsful of salt, four of ground black pepper, three table spoonsful of ground mustard, half a table spoonful of allspice, half a spoonful of cloves, six red peppers, ground fine —simmer the whole slowly, with a pint of vinegar, three or four hours— then strain it through a sieve, bottle and cork it tight. The catsup should be made in a tin utensil, and the later in the season it is made, the less liable it will be to spoil.

59. *Mushroom Catsup.*

Put a layer of fresh mushrooms in a deep dish, sprinkle a little salt over them, then put in another layer of fresh mushrooms, and salt, and so on till you get in all the mushrooms. Let them remain several days—then mash them fine, and to each quart put a table spoonful of vinegar, half a tea spoonful of black pepper, and a quarter of a tea spoonful of cloves—turn it into a stone jar, set the jar in a pot of boiling water, and let it boil two hours, then strain it without squeezing the mushrooms. Boil the juice a quarter of an hour, skim it well, let it stand a few hours to settle, then turn it off carefully through a sieve, bottle and cork it tight. Keep it in a cool place.

60. *Walnut Catsup.*

Procure the walnuts by the last of June—keep them in salt and water for a week, then bruise them, and turn boiling vinegar on them. Let them remain covered with vinegar for several days, stirring them up each day—then boil them a quarter of an hour with a little more vinegar, strain it through a thick cloth, so that none of the coarse particles of the walnuts will go through—season the vinegar highly with cloves, allspice, pepper and salt. Boil the whole a few minutes, then bottle and cork it tight. Keep it in a cool place.

61. *Curry Powder.*

Mix an ounce of ginger, one of mustard, one of pepper, three of coriander seed, the same quantity of turmeric, a quarter of an ounce of cayenne pepper, half an ounce of cardamums, and the same of cummin seed and cinnamon. Pound the whole fine, sift, and keep it in a bottle corked tight.

62. *Essence of Celery.*

Steep an ounce of celery seed in half a pint of brandy, or vinegar. A few drops of this will give a fine flavor to soups, and sauce for fowls.

63. *Soup Herb Spirit.*

Those who like a variety of herbs in soup, will find it very convenient to have the following mixture. Take when in their prime, thyme, sweet marjoram, sweet basil, and summer savory. When thoroughly dried, pound and sift them. Steep them in brandy for a fortnight, the spirit will then be fit for use.

64. *Plain Veal Soup.*

A leg of veal, after enough has been cut off for cutlets, makes a soup nearly as good as calf's head. Boil it with a cup two thirds full of rice, a pound and a half of pork—season it with salt, pepper, and sweet herbs, if you like. A little celery boiled in it gives the soup a fine flavor. Some people like onions, carrots, and parsely boiled in it. If you wish for balls in the soup, chop veal and a little raw salt pork fine, mix it with a few bread crumbs, and a couple of eggs. Season it with salt and pepper—add a little curry powder if you like, do it up into small balls, and boil them in the soup. The veal should be taken up before the soup is seasoned. Just before the soup is taken up, put in a couple of slices of toast, cut into small pieces. If you do not like your soup fat, let the liquor remain till the day after you have boiled the meat, and skim off the fat before heating the liquor. The shoulder of veal makes a good soup.

65. *Mock Turtle, or Calf's Head Soup.*

Boil the head until perfectly tender—then take it out, strain the liquor, and set it away until the next day—then skim off the fat, cut up the meat, together with the lights, and put it into the liquor, put it on the fire, and season it with salt, pepper, cloves, and mace—add onions and sweet herbs, if you like—stew it gently for half an hour. Just before you take it up, add half a pint of white wine. For the balls, chop lean veal fine, with a little salt pork, add the brains, and season it with salt, pepper, cloves, mace, sweet herbs or curry powder, make it up into balls about the size of half an egg, boil part in the soup, and fry the remainder, and put them in a dish by themselves.

66. *Beef or Black Soup.*

The shank of beef is the best part for soup—cold roast beef bones, and beef steak, make very good soup. Boil the shank four or five hours in water, enough to cover it. Half an hour before the soup is put on the table, take up the meat, thicken the soup with scorched flour, mixed with cold water, season it with salt, pepper, cloves, mace, a little walnut, or tomato catsup improves it, put in sweet herbs or herb spirit if you like. Some cooks boil onions in the soup, but as they are very disagreeable to many persons, it is better to boil and serve them up in a dish by themselves. Make force meat balls of part of the beef and pork, season them with mace, cloves, pepper, and salt, and boil them in the soup fifteen minutes.

67. *Chicken or Turkey Soup.*

The liquor that a turkey or chicken is boiled in, makes a good soup. If you do not like your soup fat, let the liquor remain till the day after the poultry has been boiled in it, then skim off the fat, set it where it will boil. If there was not any rice boiled with the meat, put in half a tea cup full, when the liquor boils, or slice up a few potatoes and put in—season it with salt and pepper, sweet herbs, and a little celery boiled in it improves it. Toast bread or crackers, and put them in the soup when you take it up.

68. *Oyster Soup.*

Separate the oysters from the liquor, to each quart of the liquor, put a pint of milk or water, set it on the fire with the oysters. Mix a heaping table spoonful of flour with a little water, and stir it into the liquor as soon as it boils. Season it with salt, pepper, and a little walnut, or butternut vinegar, if you have it, if not, common vinegar may be substituted. Put in a small lump of butter, and turn it as soon as it boils up again on to buttered toast, cut into small pieces.

69. *Pea Soup.*

If you make your soup of dry peas, soak them over night, in a warm place, using a quart of water to each quart of the peas. Early the next morning boil them an hour. Boil with them a tea spoonful of saleratus, eight or ten minutes, then take them out of the water they were soaking in, put them into fresh water, with a pound of salt pork, and boil it till the peas are soft, which will be in the course of three or four hours. Green peas for soup require no soaking, and boiling only long enough to have the pork get thoroughly cooked, which will be in the course of an hour.

70. *Portable Soup.*

Take beef or veal soup, and let it get perfectly cold, then skim off every particle of the grease. Set it on the fire, and let it boil till of a thick glutinous consistence. Care should be taken that it does not burn. Season it highly with salt, pepper, cloves and mace—add a little wine or brandy, and then turn it on to earthen platters. It should not be more than a quarter of an inch in thickness. Let it remain until cold, then cut it in pieces three inches square, set them in the sun to dry, turning them frequently. When perfectly dry, put them in an earthen or tin vessel, having a layer of white paper between each layer. These, if the directions are strictly attended to, will keep good a long time. Whenever you wish to make a soup of them, nothing more is necessary, than to put a quart of water to one of the cakes, and heat it very hot.

71. *To Boil Eggs.*

They should be put into boiling water, and if you wish to have them soft, boil them only three minutes. If you wish to have them hard enough to cut in slices, boil them five minutes. Another way which is very nice, is to break the shells, and drop the eggs into a pan of scalding hot water, let it stand till the white has set, then put the pan on a moderate fire, when the water boils up, the eggs are cooked sufficiently. Eggs look very prettily cooked in this way, the yelk being just visible through the white. If you do not use the eggs for a garnish, serve them up with burnt butter. See receipt for making, [No. 42](#).

72. *Omelet.*

Beat the eggs to a froth, and to a dozen of eggs put three ounces of finely minced boiled ham, beef, or veal; if the latter meat is used, add a little salt. Melt a quarter of a pound of butter, mix a little of it with the eggs—it should be just lukewarm. Set the remainder of the butter on the fire, in a frying or tin pan, when quite hot, turn in the eggs beaten to a froth, stir them until they begin to set. When brown on the under side, it is sufficiently cooked. The omelet should be cooked on a moderate fire, and in a pan small enough, to have the omelet an inch thick. When you take them up, lay a flat dish on them, then turn the pan upside down.

73. *Poached Eggs.*

Break the eggs into a pan, beat them to a froth, then put them into a buttered tin pan, set the pan on a few coals, put in a small lump of butter, a little salt, let them cook very slowly, stirring them constantly till they become quite thick, then turn them on to buttered toast.

74. *Directions for Broiling, Boiling and Frying Fish.*

Fish for boiling or broiling are the best the day after they are caught. They should be cleaned when first caught, washed in cold water, and half a tea cup of salt sprinkled on the inside of them. If they are to be broiled, sprinkle pepper on the inside of them—keep them in a cool place. When fish is broiled, the bars of the gridiron should be rubbed over with a little butter, and the inside of the fish put towards the fire, and not turned till the fish is nearly cooked through—then butter the skin side, and turn it over—fish should be broiled slowly. When fresh fish is to be boiled, it should either be laid on a fish strainer, or sewed up in a cloth—if not, it is very difficult to take it out of the pot without breaking. Put the fish into cold water, with the back bone down. To eight or ten pounds of fish, put half of a small tea cup of salt. Boil the fish until you can draw out one of the fins easily—most kinds of fish will boil sufficiently in the course of twenty or thirty minutes, some kinds will boil in less time. Some cooks do not put their fish into the water till it boils, but it is not a good plan, as the outside gets cooked too much, and breaks to pieces before the inside is sufficiently done. Fish for frying, after being cleaned and washed, should be put into a cloth to have it absorb the moisture. They should be dried perfectly, and a little flour rubbed over them. No salt should be put on them, if you wish to have them brown well. For five or six pounds of fish, fry three or four slices of salt pork—when brown, take them up, and if they do not make fat sufficient to fry the fish in, add a little lard. When the fish are fried enough, take them up, and for good plain gravy, mix two or three tea spoonsful of flour with a little water, and stir it into the fat the fish was fried in—put in a little butter, pepper, and salt, if you wish to have the gravy rich—add spices, catsup and wine—turn the gravy over the fish. Boiled fish should be served up with drawn butter, or liver sauce, (see directions for making each, Nos. 41 and 51.) Fish, when put on the platter, should not be laid over each other if it can be avoided, as the steam from the under ones makes those on the top so moist, that they will break to pieces when served out.

Great care and punctuality is necessary in cooking fish. If not done sufficiently, or if done too much, they are not good. They should be eaten as soon as cooked. For a garnish to the fish, use parsely, a lemon, or eggs boiled hard, and cut in slices.

75. *Chowder.*

Fry three or four slices of pork till brown—cut each of your fish into five or six slices, flour, and put a layer of them in your pork fat, sprinkle on pepper and a little salt—add cloves, mace, and sliced onions if you like—lay on several bits of your fried pork, and crackers previously soaked soft in cold water. This process repeat till you get in all the fish, then turn on water enough to just cover them—put on a heated bake pan lid. When the fish have stewed about twenty minutes, take them up, and mix a couple of tea spoonsful of flour with a little water, and stir it into the gravy, also, a little butter and pepper. Half a pint of white wine, spices, and catsup, will improve it. Bass and cod make the best chowder—black fish and clams make tolerably good ones. The hard part of the clams should be cut off, and thrown away.

76. *Stuffed and Baked Fish.*

Soak bread in cold water till soft—drain off the water, mash the bread fine, mix it with a table spoonful of melted butter, a little pepper and salt—a couple of raw eggs makes the dressing cut smoother—add spices if you like. Fill the fish, with the dressing, sew it up, put a tea cup of water in your bake pan, and a small piece of butter—lay in the fish, bake it from forty to fifty minutes. Fresh cod, bass, and shad, are suitable fish for baking.

77. *Codfish.*

Fresh cod is good boiled, fried, or made into a chowder. It is too dry a fish to broil. Salt cod should be soaked in lukewarm water till the skin will come off easily—then take up the fish, scrape off the skin, and put it in fresh water, and set it on a very moderate fire, where it will keep warm without boiling, as it hardens by boiling. It takes between three and four hours to cook it soft—serve it up with drawn butter. Cold salt codfish is nice minced fine, and mixed with mashed potatoes, and warmed up, with just water enough to moisten it, and considerable butter. It makes a nice dish for breakfast, prepared in the following manner. Pull the fish into small pieces, soak it an hour in warm water, then drain off the water, put a little milk and butter to it, stew it a few minutes, and serve it up with soft boiled eggs.

78. *Cod Sounds and Tongues.*

Soak them four or five hours in lukewarm water—then take them out of the water, scrape off the skin, cut them once in two, and stew them in a little milk. Just before they are taken up, stir in butter, and a little flour.

79. *Halibut.*

Is nice cut in slices, salted and peppered, and broiled or fried. The fins and thick part is good boiled.

80. *Striped and Sea Bass.*

Bass are good fried, boiled, broiled, or made into a chowder.

81. *Black Fish.*

Are the best boiled or fried—they will do to broil, but are not so good as cooked in any other way.

82. *Shad.*

Fresh shad are good baked or boiled, but better broiled. For broiling, they should have a good deal of salt and pepper sprinkled on the inside of them, and remain several hours before broiling. The spawn and liver are good boiled or fried. Salt shad and mackerel, for broiling, should be soaked ten or twelve hours in cold water. Salt shad, for boiling, need not be soaked only long enough to get off the scales, without you like them quite fresh—if so, turn boiling water on them, and let them soak in it an hour—then put them into fresh boiling water, and boil them twenty minutes. To pickle shad, mix one pound of sugar, a peck of rock salt, two quarts of blown salt, and a quarter of a pound of salt-petre. Allow this quantity to every twenty-five shad. Put a layer of the mixture at the bottom of the keg, then a layer of cleaned shad, with the skin side down. Sprinkle on another layer of salt, sugar, and salt-petre, and so on till you get in all the shad. Lay a heavy weight on the shad, to keep it under the brine. If the juice of the shad does not run out so as to form brine sufficient to cover them, in the course of a week, make a little brine, and turn on to them.

83. *Sturgeons.*

Sturgeons are good boiled or baked, but better fried. Before baking it, boil it about fifteen minutes, to extract the strong oily taste, and when baked, to eight or ten pounds of it put a quart of water into the pan, and bake it till tender. (See directions for baking fish, No. 76.) The part next to the tail is the best for baking or frying. Sturgeons are very nice, cooked in the following manner. Cut it in slices nearly an inch thick—fry a few slices of pork—when brown, take them up, and put in the sturgeon. When a good brown color, take them up, and stir in a little flour and water, mixed smoothly together. Season the gravy with salt, pepper, and catsup—stir in a little butter, and wine if you like, then put back the sturgeon, and let it stew a few minutes in the gravy. While the sturgeon is cooking, make force meat balls of part of the sturgeon and salt pork—fry and use them as a garnish for the fish.

84. *Fish Cakes.*

Cold boiled fresh fish, or salt codfish, is nice minced fine, with potatoes, moistened with a little water, and a little butter put in, done up into cakes of the size of common biscuit, and fried brown in pork fat or butter.

85. *Fish Force Meat Balls.*

Take a little uncooked fish, chop it fine, together with a little raw salt pork, mix it with one or two raw eggs, a few bread crumbs, and season the whole with pepper and spices. Add a little catsup if you like—do them up into small balls, and fry them till brown.

86. *Lobsters and Crabs.*

Put them into boiling water, and boil them from half to three quarters of an hour, according to their size. Boil half a tea cup of salt with every four pounds of the fish. When cold, crack the shell, and take out the meat, taking care to extract the blue veins, and what is called the lady in the lobster, as they are very unhealthy. If the fish are not eaten cold, warm them up with a little water, vinegar, salt, pepper, and butter. The following way of dressing lobsters looks very prettily. Pick out the spawn and red chord, mash them fine, rub them through a sieve, put in a little butter and salt. Cut the lobsters into squares, and warm it, together with the spawn, over a moderate fire. When hot, take it up, and garnish it with parsely. The chord and spawn are a handsome garnish for any kind of fish.

87. *Scollops.*

Are nice boiled, and then fried, or boiled and pickled, in the same manner as oysters. Take them out of the shells—when boiled, pick out the hearts, and throw the rest away, as the heart is the only part that is healthy to eat. Dip the hearts in flour, and fry them in lard till brown. The hearts are good stewed, with a little water, butter, salt, and pepper.

88. *Eels.*

Eels, if very large, are best split open, cut into short pieces, and seasoned with salt and pepper, and broiled several hours after they have been salted. They are good cut into small strips, and laid in a deep dish, with bits of salt pork, seasoned with salt and pepper, and covered with pounded rusked bread, then baked half an hour. Small eels are the best fried.

89. *Trout.*

Trout are good boiled, broiled, or fried—they are also good stewed a few minutes, with bits of salt pork, butter, and a little water. Trout, as well as all other kinds of fresh water fish, are apt to have an earthy taste—to remove it, soak them in salt and water a few minutes, after they are cleaned.

90. *Clams.*

Wash and put them in a pot, with just water enough to prevent the shells burning at the bottom of the pot. Heat them till the shells open—take the clams out of them, and warm them with a little of the clam liquor, a little salt, butter, and pepper. Toast a slice or two of bread, soak it in the clam liquor, lay it in a deep dish, and turn the clams on to it. For clam pancakes, mix flour and milk together to form a thick batter—some cooks use the clam liquor, but it does not make the pancakes as light as the milk. To each pint of the milk, put a couple of eggs, and a few clams—they are good taken out of the shells without stewing, and chopped fine, or stewed, and put into the cakes whole. Very large long clams are good taken out of the shells without stewing, and broiled.

91. *Stewed Oysters.*

Strain the oyster liquor, rinse the bits of shells off the oysters, then turn the liquor back on to the oysters, and put them in a stew pan—set them where they will boil up, then turn them on to buttered toast—salt, pepper, and butter them to your taste. Some cooks add a little walnut catsup, or vinegar. The oysters should not be cooked till just before they are to be eaten.

92. *To Fry Oysters.*

Take those that are large, dip them in beaten eggs, and then in flour, or fine bread crumbs—fry them in lard, till of a light brown. They are a nice garnish for fish. They will keep good for several months if fried when first caught, salted and peppered, then put into a bottle, and corked tight. Whenever they are to be eaten, warm them in a little water.

93. *Oyster Pancakes.*

Mix equal quantities of milk and oyster juice together. To a pint of the liquor when mixed, put a pint of wheat flour, a few oysters, a couple of eggs, and a little salt. Drop it by the large spoonful into hot lard.

94. *Oyster Pie.*

Line a deep pie plate with pie crust—fill it with dry pieces of bread, cover it over with puff paste—bake it till a light brown, either in a quick oven or bake pan. Have the oysters just stewed by the time the crust is done—take off the upper crust, remove the pieces of bread, put in the oysters, season them with salt, pepper, and butter. A little walnut catsup improves the pie, but is not essential—cover it with the crust.

95. *Scolloped Oysters.*

Pound rusked bread or crackers fine—butter scollop shells or tins, sprinkle on the bread crumbs, then put in a layer of oysters, a small lump of butter, pepper, salt, and a little of the oyster juice—then put on another layer of crumbs and oysters, and so on till the shells are filled, having a layer of crumbs at the top. Bake them till a light brown.

96. *Potatoes.*

The best way to cook Irish potatoes, is to pare and put them in a pot, with just boiling water enough to prevent their burning, and a little salt. Cover them tight, and let them stew till you can stick a fork through them easily. If any water remains in the pot, turn it off, put the pot where it will keep moderately warm, and let the potatoes steam a few moments longer. The easiest way to cook them, is to put them in boiling water, with the skins on, and boiled constantly till done. They will not be mealy if they lie soaking in the water without boiling. They are more mealy to peel them as soon as tender, and then put back in the pot without any water, and set in a warm place where they will steam, with the lid of the pot off. Old and poor potatoes are best boiled till soft, then peeled and mashed fine, with a little salt, butter, and very little milk put in—then put into a dish, smoothed over with a knife, a little flour sprinkled over it, and put where it will brown. Cold mashed, or whole boiled potatoes, are nice cut in slices, and fried with just butter or lard enough to prevent their burning. When brown on both sides, take them up, salt and butter them. Most potatoes will boil in the course of half an hour—new ones will boil in less time. Sweet potatoes are better baked than boiled.

97. *Potato Snow Balls.*

Take the white mealy kind of potatoes—pare them, and put them into just boiling water enough to cover them—add a little salt. When boiled tender, drain off the water, and let them steam till they break to pieces—take them up, put two or three at a time compactly together in a strong cloth, and press them tight, in the form of a ball—then lay them in your potatoe dish carefully, so as not to fall apart.

98. *Turnips.*

White turnips require about as much boiling as potatoes. When tender, take them up, peel and mash them—season them with a little salt and butter. Yellow turnips require about two hours boiling—if very large, split them in two. The tops of white turnips make a good salad.

99. *Beets.*

Beets should not be cut or scraped before they are boiled, or the juice will run out, and make them insipid. In summer, they will boil in an hour—in winter, it takes three hours to boil them tender. The tops in summer are good boiled for greens. Boiled beets cut in slices, and put in cold spiced vinegar for several days, are very nice.

100. *Parsnips and Carrots.*

Wash them, and split them in two—lay them in a stew pan, with the flat side down, turn on boiling water enough to cover them—boil them till tender, then take them up, and take off the skin, and butter them. Many cooks boil them whole, but it is not a good plan, as the outside gets done too much, before the inside is cooked sufficiently. Cold boiled parsnips are good cut in slices, and fried brown.

101. *Onions.*

Peel and put them in boiling milk, (water will do, but it is not as good.) When boiled tender, take them up, salt them, and turn a little melted butter over them.

102. *Artichokes.*

Scrape and put them in boiling water, with a table spoonful of salt to a couple of dozen. When boiled tender, (which will be in about two hours,) take them up, salt and butter each one.

103. *Squashes.*

Summer squashes, if very young, may be boiled whole—if not, they should be pared, quartered, and the seeds taken out. When boiled very tender, take them up, put them in a strong cloth, and press out all the water—mash them, salt and butter them to your taste. The neck part of the winter squash is the best. Cut it in narrow strips, take off the rind, and boil the squash in salt and water till tender—then drain off the water, and let the pumpkin steam over a moderate fire for ten or twelve minutes. It is good not mashed—if mashed, add a little butter.

104. *Cabbage and Cauliflowers.*

Trim off the loose leaves of the cabbage, cut the stalky in quarters, to the heart of the cabbage—boil it an hour. If not boiled with corned beef, put a little salt in the water in which they are boiled. White cauliflowers are the best. Take off the outside leaves, cut the stalk close to the leaves, let them lie in salt and cold water for half an hour before boiling them—boil them fifteen or twenty minutes, according to their size. Milk and water is the best to boil them in, but clear water does very well. Put a little salt in the pot in which they are boiled.

105. *Asparagus.*

Cut the white part of the stalks off, and throw it away—cut the lower part of the stalks in thin slices if tough, and boil them eight or ten minutes before the upper part is put in. Lay the remainder compactly together, tie it carefully in small bundles, and boil it from fifteen to twenty minutes, according to its age. Boil a little salt with them, and a quarter of a tea spoonful of saleratus, to two or three quarts of water, to preserve their fresh green color. Just before your asparagus is done, toast a slice of bread, moisten it with a little of the asparagus liquor, lay it in your asparagus dish, and butter it—then take up the asparagus carefully with a skimmer, and lay it on the toast, take off the string, salt it, and turn a little melted butter over the whole.

106. *Peas.*

Peas should be put into boiling water, with salt and saleratus, in the proportion of a quarter of a tea spoonful of saleratus to half a peck of peas. Boil them from fifteen to thirty minutes, according to their age and kind. When boiled tender, take them out of the water with a skimmer, salt and butter them to the taste. Peas to be good should be fresh gathered, and not shelled till just before they are cooked.

107. *Sweet Corn.*

Corn is much sweeter to be boiled on the cob. If made into sucatosh, cut it from the cobs, and boil it with Lima beans, and a few slices of salt pork. It requires boiling from fifteen to thirty minutes, according to its age.

108. *To cook various kinds of Beans.*

French beans should have the strings taken off—if old, the edges should be cut off, and the beans cut through the middle. Boil them with a little salt, from twenty-five to forty minutes, according to their age. A little saleratus boiled with them preserves their green color, and makes them more healthy. Salt and butter them when taken up. Lima beans can be kept the year round, by being perfectly dried when fresh gathered in the pods, or being put without drying into a keg, with a layer of salt to each layer of beans, having a layer of salt at the bottom of the keg. Cover them tight, and keep them in a cool place. Whenever you wish to cook them, soak them over night, in cold water—shell and boil them, with a little saleratus. White beans for baking, should be picked over carefully to get out the colored and bad ones. Wash and soak them over night in a pot, set where they will keep lukewarm. There should be about three quarts of water to three pints of the beans. The next morning set them where they will boil, with a tea spoonful of saleratus. When they have boiled four or five minutes, take them up with a skimmer. Put them in a baking pot. Gash a pound of pork, and put it down in the pot, so as to have the beans cover all but the upper surface—turn in cold water till you can just see it at the top. They will bake in a hot oven, in the course of three hours—but they are better to remain in it five or six hours. Beans are good prepared in the same manner as for baking, and stewed several hours without baking.

109. *Greens.*

White mustard, spinach, water cresses, dandelions, and the leaves and roots of very small beets, are the best greens. Boil them with a little salt and saleratus in the water. If not fresh and plump, soak them in salt and water half an hour before cooking them. When they are boiled enough, they will sink to the bottom of the pot.

110. *Salads.*

To be in perfection, salads should be fresh gathered, and kept in cold water for an hour before they are put on the table. The water should be drained from them, and if you have not any salad oil, melt a little butter and put it in a separate dish—if turned over the salad, it will not be crispy.

111. *Cucumbers.*

To be healthy they should not be picked longer than a day before they are to be eaten. They should be kept in cold water, and fifteen or twenty minutes before they are to be eaten, pare and slice them into fresh cold water, to take out the slimy matter. Just before they are put on the table, drain off the water. Put them in a deep dish; sprinkle on a good deal of salt and pepper—cover them with vinegar. Cucumbers are thought by many people to be very unhealthy, but if properly prepared, they will not be found to be any more unwholesome than most other summer vegetables.

112. *To stew Mushrooms.*

Cut off the lower part of the stem, as it is apt to have an earthy taste. Peel and put them in a saucepan, with just water enough at the bottom, to prevent their burning to the pan. Put in a little salt, and shake them occasionally while stewing, to prevent their burning. When they have stewed quite tender, put in a little butter and pepper—add spices and wine if you like. They should stew very slowly till tender, and not be seasoned till just before they are taken up. Serve them up on buttered toast.

113. *Egg Plant.*

Boil them a few moments to extract the bitter taste—then cut them in thick slices; sprinkle a little salt between each slice. Let them lie half an hour—then fry them till brown in lard.

114. *Celeriac.*

This is an excellent vegetable, but is little known. The stalks of it can hardly be distinguished from celery, and it is much easier cultivated. The roots are nice boiled tender, cut in thin slices, and put in soup or meat pies; or cooked in the following manner, and eaten with meat. Scrape and cut them in slices. Boil them till very tender—then drain off the water. Sprinkle a little salt over them—turn in milk enough to cover them. When they have stewed about four or five minutes, turn them into a dish, and add a little butter.

115. *Salsify or Vegetable Oyster.*

The best way to cook it is to parboil it, (after scraping off the outside,) then cut it in slices, dip it into a beaten egg, and fine bread crumbs, and fry it in lard. It is very good boiled, then stewed a few minutes in milk, with a little butter and salt. Another way which is very good, is to make a batter of wheat flour, milk and eggs; cut the Salsify in thin slices, (after having been boiled tender,) put them into the batter with a little salt; drop this mixture into hot fat, by the large spoonful. When a light brown, they are cooked sufficiently.

116. *Tomatoes.*

If very ripe will skin easily; if not, pour scalding water on them, and let them remain in it four or five minutes. Peel and put them in a stew pan, with a table spoonful of water, if not very juicy; if so, no water will be required. Put in a little salt, and stew them for half an hour; then turn them into a deep dish with buttered toast. Another way of cooking them, which is considered very nice by epicures, is to put them in a deep dish, with fine bread crumbs, crackers pounded fine, a layer of each alternately; put small bits of butter, a little salt, and pepper on each layer—some cooks add a little nutmeg and sugar. Have a layer of bread crumbs on the top. Bake it three quarters of an hour.

117. *Gumbo.*

Take an equal quantity of young tender ocra chopped fine, and ripe tomatoes skinned, an onion cut into slices, a small lump of butter, a little salt and pepper. Put the whole in a stew pan, with a table spoonful of water, and stew it till tender.

118. *Southern manner of Boiling Rice.*

Pick over the rice, rinse it in cold water a number of times, to get it perfectly clean; drain off the water, then put it in a pot of boiling water, with a little salt. Allow as much as a quart of water to a tea-cup of rice, as it absorbs the water very much while boiling. Boil it seventeen minutes; then turn the water off very close; set the pot over a few coals, and let it steam fifteen minutes with the lid of the pot off. The beauty of rice boiled in this way, is, that each kernel stands out by itself, while it is quite tender. Great care is necessary to be used in the time of boiling and steaming it, as a few moments variation in the time, makes a great deal of difference in the looks of it. The water should boil hard when the rice is put in, and not suffered to stop boiling, till turned off to have the rice steamed. The water that the rice is boiled in, makes good starch for muslin, if boiled a few minutes by itself.

119. *Directions for Pickling.*

Vinegar for pickling should be good, but not of the sharpest kind. Brass utensils should be used for pickling. They should be thoroughly cleaned before using, and no vinegar should be allowed to cool in them, as the rust formed by so doing is very poisonous. Boil alum and salt in the vinegar, in the proportion of half a tea cup of salt, and a table spoonful of alum, to three gallons of vinegar. Stone and wooden vessels are the only kinds of utensils that are good to keep pickles in. Vessels that have had any grease in will not do for pickles, as no washing will kill the grease that the pot has absorbed. All kinds of pickles should be stirred up occasionally. If there is any soft ones among them, they should be taken out, the vinegar scalded, and turned back while hot—if very weak, throw it away, and use fresh vinegar. Whenever any scum rises, the vinegar needs scalding. If you do not wish to have all your pickles spiced, it is a good plan to keep a stone pot of spiced vinegar by itself, and put in a few of your pickles a short time before they are to be eaten.

120. *To Pickle Peppers.*

Procure those that are fresh and green. If you do not like them very fiery, cut a small slit in them, and take the seeds out carefully with a small knife, so as not to mangle the pepper. Soak them in salt and water, eight or nine days, changing the water each day. Keep them in a warm place. If you like them stuffed, chop white cabbage fine, season it highly with cloves, cinnamon, mace, and fill the peppers with it—add nasturtions if you like—sew them up carefully, and put them in cold spiced vinegar. Tomatoes when very small and green are good pickled with the peppers.

121. *Mangoes.*

Procure muskmelons as late in the season as possible—if pickled early, they are not apt to keep well. Cut a small piece from the side that lies upon the ground while growing, take out the seeds, and if the citron or nutmeg melons are used for mangoes, the rough part should be scraped off. The long common muskmelons make the best mangoes. Soak the melons in salt and water, three or four days; then take them out of the water; sprinkle on the inside of the melons, powdered cloves, pepper, nutmeg; fill them with small strips of horseradish, cinnamon, and small string beans. Flag root, nasturtions, and radish tops, are also nice to fill them with. Fill the crevices with American mustard seed. Put back the pieces of melon that were cut off, and bind the melon up tight with white cotton cloth, sew it on. Lay the melons in a stone jar, with the part that the covers are on, up. Put into vinegar for the mangoes, alum, salt and peppercorns, in the same proportion as for cucumbers—heat it scalding hot, then turn it on to the melons. Barberries or radish tops pickled in bunches, are a pretty garnish for mangoes. The barberries preserve their natural color best by being first dried. Whenever you wish to use them, turn boiling vinegar on them, and let them lie in it several hours to swell out.

122. *To Pickle Butternuts and Walnuts.*

The nuts for pickling should be gathered as early as July, unless the season is very backward. When a pin will go through them easily, they are young enough to pickle. Soak them in salt and water a week—then drain it off. Rub them with a cloth, to get off the roughness. To a gallon of vinegar put a tea-cup of salt, a table-spoonful of powdered cloves and mace, mixed together, half an ounce of allspice, and peppercorns. Boil the vinegar and spices, and turn it while hot on to the nuts. In the course of a week, scald the vinegar, and turn it back on them while hot. They will be fit to eat in the course of a fortnight.

123. *Peaches and Apricots.*

Take those of a full growth, but perfectly green, put them in salt and water, strong enough to bear up an egg. When they have been in a week, take them out, and wipe them carefully with a soft cloth. Lay them in a pickle jar. Put to a gallon of vinegar half an ounce of cloves, the same quantity of peppercorns, sliced ginger and mustard seed—add salt, and boil the vinegar—then turn it on to the peaches scalding hot. Turn the vinegar from them several times. Heat it scalding hot, and turn it back while hot.

124. *To Pickle Cabbages and Cauliflowers.*

Purple cabbages are the best for pickling. Pull off the loose leaves, quarter the cabbages, put them in a keg, and sprinkle a great deal of salt, on each one—let them remain five or six days. To a gallon of vinegar put an ounce of mace, one of peppercorns and cinnamon, (cloves and allspice improve the taste of the cabbages, but they turn it a dark color.) Heat the vinegar scalding hot, put in a little alum, and turn it while hot on to the cabbages—the salt should remain that was sprinkled on the cabbages. Turn the vinegar from the cabbages six or seven times—heat it scalding hot, and turn it back while hot, to make them tender. Cauliflowers are pickled in the same manner. Cauliflowers cut into bunches, and pickled with beet roots sliced, look very prettily.

125. *East India Pickle.*

Chop cabbage fine, leaving out the stalks, together with three or four onions, a root of horseradish, and a couple of green peppers to each cabbage. Soak the whole in salt and water three or four days. Spice some vinegar very strong with mace, cloves, allspice and cinnamon. Heat it scalding hot—add alum and salt, and turn it on to the cabbage, onions and pepper, which should previously have all the brine drained from them. This pickle will be fit to eat in the course of three or four weeks.

126. *French Beans and Radish Pods.*

Gather them while quite small and tender. Keep them in salt and water, till you get through collecting them—changing the water as often as once in four or five days. Then scald them with hot salt and water, let them lie in it till cool, then turn on hot vinegar spiced with peppercorns, mace and allspice. The radish top, if pickled in small bunches, are a pretty garnish for other pickles.

127. *Nasturtion.*

Take them when small and green—put them in salt and water—change the water once in three days. When you have done collecting the nasturtions, turn off the brine, and pour on scalding hot vinegar.

128. *Samphire.*

Procure samphire that is fresh and green—let it lay in salt for three days—then take it out, and for a peck of samphire spice a gallon of vinegar with a couple of dozen of peppercorns—add half a tea-cup of salt—heat the vinegar scalding hot, and turn it on to the samphire while hot—cover it close. In the course of ten days, turn the vinegar from the samphire, heat it scalding hot, and turn it back.

129. *Onions.*

Peel and boil them in milk and water ten minutes. To a gallon of vinegar put half an ounce of cinnamon and mace, a quarter of an ounce of cloves, a small tea-cup of salt, and half an ounce of alum. Heat the vinegar, together with the spices, scalding hot, and turn it on to the onions, which should previously have the water and milk drained from them. Cover them tight till cold.

130. *Artichokes.*

Soak the artichokes in salt and water, for several days, then drain and rub them till you get all the skin off. Turn boiling vinegar on them, with salt, alum, and peppercorns in it, in the same proportion as for cucumbers. Let them remain a week, then turn off the vinegar, scald it, and turn it back while hot on to the artichokes. Continue to turn boiling vinegar on to the artichokes till thoroughly pickled.

131. *Cucumbers.*

Gather those that are small and green, and of a quick growth. Turn boiling water on them as soon as picked. Let them remain in it four or five hours, then put them in cold vinegar, with alum and salt, in the proportion of a table spoonful of the former and a tea cup of the latter, to every gallon of vinegar. When you have done collecting the cucumbers for pickling, turn the vinegar from the cucumbers, scald and skim it till clear, then put in the pickles, let them scald without boiling, for a few minutes; then turn them while hot into the vessel you intend to keep them in. A few peppers, or peppercorns, improve the taste of the cucumbers. Cucumbers to be brittle need scalding several times. If the vinegar is weak, it should be thrown away, and fresh put to the cucumbers, with more alum and salt. Another method of pickling cucumbers, which is good, is to put them in salt and water, as you pick them—changing the salt and water once in three or four days. When you have done collecting your cucumbers for pickling, take them out of the salt and water, turn on scalding hot vinegar, with alum, salt and peppercorns in it.

132. *Gherkins.*

Put them in strong brine—keep them in a warm place. When they turn yellow, drain off the brine, and turn hot vinegar on them. Let them remain in it till they turn green, keeping them in a warm place. Then turn off the vinegar—add fresh scalding hot vinegar, spiced with mace, allspice, and peppercorns—add alum and salt, in the same proportion as for cucumbers.

133. *To Pickle Oysters.*

Take the oysters from the liquor, strain and boil it. Rinse the oysters, if there are any bits of the shells attached to them. Put them into the liquor while boiling. Boil them one minute, then take them out of it, and to the liquor put a few peppercorns, cloves, and a blade or two of mace—add a little salt, and the same quantity of vinegar as oyster juice. Let the whole boil fifteen minutes, then turn it on to the oysters. If you wish to keep the oysters for a number of weeks, bottle and cork them tight as soon as cold.

134. *To Pickle Mushrooms.*

Peel and stew them, with just water enough to prevent their sticking at the bottom of the pan. Shake them occasionally, to prevent their burning. When tender, take them up, and put them in scalding hot vinegar, spiced with mace, cloves, and peppercorns—add a little salt. Bottle and cork them tight, if you wish to keep them long.

135. *Wheat Bread.*

For six common sized loaves of bread, take three pints of boiling water, and mix it with five or six quarts of flour. When thoroughly mixed, add three pints of cold water. Stir it till the whole of the dough is of the same temperature. When lukewarm, stir in half a pint of family yeast, (if brewers' yeast is used, a less quantity will answer,) a table-spoonful of salt, knead in flour till stiff enough to mould up, and free from lumps. The more the bread is kneaded, the better it will be. Cover it over with a thick cloth, and if the weather is cold, set it near a fire. To ascertain when it has risen, cut it through the middle with a knife—if full of small holes like a sponge, it is sufficiently light for baking. It should be baked as soon as light. If your bread should get sour before you are ready to bake it, dissolve two or more tea-spoonsful of saleratus (according to the acidity of it) in a tea-cup of milk or water, strain it on to the dough, work it in well—then cut off enough for a loaf of bread—mould it up well, slash it on both sides, to prevent its cracking when baked—put it in a buttered tin-pan. The bread should stand ten or twelve minutes in the pans before baking it. If you like your bread baked a good deal, let it stand in the oven an hour and a half. When the wheat is grown, it makes better bread to wet the flour entirely with boiling water. It should remain till cool before working in the yeast. Some cooks have an idea that it kills the life of the flour to scald it, but it is a mistaken idea—it is sweeter for it, and will keep good much longer. Bread made in this way is nearly as good as that which is wet with milk. Care must be taken not to put the yeast in when the dough is hot, as it will scald it, and prevents its rising. Most ovens require heating an hour and a half for bread. A brisk fire should be kept up, and the doors of the room should be kept shut, if the weather is cold. Pine and ash, mixed together, or birch-wood, is the best for heating an oven. To ascertain if your oven is of the right temperature, when cleaned, throw in a little flour; if it browns in the course of a minute, it is sufficiently hot; if it turns black directly, wait several minutes, before putting in the things that are to be baked. If the oven does not bake well, set in a furnace of live coals.

136. *Sponge Bread.*

For four loaves of bread, take three quarts of wheat flour, and the same quantity of boiling water—mix them well together. Let it remain till lukewarm, then add a tea-cup full of family, or half a tea-cup of distillery yeast. Set it in a warm place to rise. When light, knead in flour till stiff enough to mould up, then let it stand till risen again, before moulding it up.

137. *Rye Bread.*

Wet up rye flour with lukewarm milk, (water will do to wet it with, but it will not make the bread so good.) Put in the same proportion of yeast as for wheat bread. For four or five loaves of bread, put in a couple of tea-spoonsful of salt. A couple of table-spoonsful of melted butter makes the crust more tender. It should not be kneaded as stiff as wheat bread, or it will be hard when baked. When light, take it out into pans, without moulding it up—let it remain in them about twenty minutes, before baking.

138. *Brown Bread.*

Brown bread is made by scalding Indian meal, and stirring into it, when lukewarm, about the same quantity of rye flour as Indian meal—add yeast and salt in the same proportion as for other kinds of bread. Bake it between two and three hours.

139. *Indian Bread.*

Mix Indian meal with cold water, stir it into boiling water, let it boil half an hour—stir in a little salt, take it from the fire, let it remain till lukewarm, then stir in yeast and Indian meal, to render it of the consistency of unbaked rye dough. When light, take it out into buttered pans, let it remain a few minutes, then bake it two hours and a half.

140. *Potato Bread.*

Boil the potatoes very soft, then peel and mash them fine. Put in salt, and very little butter—then rub them with the flour—wet the flour with lukewarm water—then work in the yeast, and flour till stiff to mould up. It will rise quicker than common wheat bread, and should be baked as soon as risen, as it turns sour very soon. The potatoes that the bread is made of should be mealy, and mixed with the flour in the proportion of one-third of potatoes to two-thirds of flour.

141. *Rice Bread.*

Boil a pint of rice till soft—then mix it with a couple of quarts of rice or wheat flour. When cool, add half a tea-cup of yeast, a little salt, and milk to render it of the consistency of rye bread. When light, bake it in small buttered pans.

142. *French Rolls.*

Turn a quart of lukewarm milk on to a quart of flour. Melt a couple of ounces of butter, and put to the milk and flour, together with a couple of eggs, and a tea-spoonful of salt. When cool, stir in half a tea-cup of yeast, and flour to make it stiff enough to mould up. Put it in a warm place. When light, do it up into small rolls—lay the rolls on flat buttered tins—let them remain twenty minutes before baking.

143. *Yeast.*

Boil a small handful of hops in a couple of quarts of water. When the strength is obtained from them, strain the liquor—put it back on the fire—take a little of the liquor, and mix smoothly with three heaping table-spoonsful of wheat flour—stir it into the liquor when it boils. Let it boil five or six minutes—take it from the fire. When lukewarm, stir in a tea-cup of yeast—keep it in a warm place till risen. When of a frothy appearance, it is sufficiently light. Add a table-spoonful of salt, turn it into a jar, and cover it tight. Some people keep yeast in bottles, but they are apt to burst—some use jugs, but they cannot be cleaned so easily as jars. Whenever your yeast gets sour, the jar should be thoroughly cleaned before fresh is put in—if not cleaned, it will spoil the fresh yeast. Yeast made in this manner will keep good a fortnight in warm weather; in cold weather longer. If your yeast appears to be a little changed, add a little saleratus to it before you mix it with your bread. If it does not foam well, when put in, it is too stale to use. Milk yeast makes sweeter bread than any other kind of yeast, but it will not keep good long. It is very nice to make biscuit of. Take half the quantity of milk you need for your biscuit—set it in a warm place, with a little flour, and a tea-spoonful of salt. When light, mix it with the rest of the milk, and use it directly for the biscuit. It takes a pint of this yeast for five or six loaves of bread. Another method of making yeast, which is very good, is to take about half a pound of your bread dough, when risen, and roll it out thin, and dry it. When you wish to make bread, put a quart of lukewarm milk to it, set it near the fire to rise—when light, scald the flour, and let it be till lukewarm—then add the yeast and salt. This will raise the bread in the course of an hour. The dough will need a little fresh hop liquor put to it, in the course of three or four times baking. Potato yeast makes very nice bread, but the yeast does not keep good as long as when made without them. It is made in the following manner: boil a couple of good, sized potatoes soft—peel and rub them through a sieve—put to it a couple of table-spoonsful of wheat flour, and a quart of hot hop tea—when lukewarm, stir in half a tea-cup of yeast—when light, put in a couple of tea-spoonsful of salt, put it in your yeast-jar, and cover it up tight.

144. *Yeast Cakes.*

Stir into a pint of good lively yeast a table-spoonful of salt, and rye or wheat flour to make a thick batter. When risen, stir in Indian meal till of the right consistency to roll out. When risen again, roll them out very thin, cut them into cakes with a tumbler, and dry them in the shade in clear windy weather. Care must be taken to keep them from the sun, or they will ferment. When perfectly dry, tie them up in a bag, and keep them in a cool dry place. To raise four or five loaves of bread, take one of these cakes, and put to it a little lukewarm milk or water. When dissolved, stir in a couple of table-spoonsful of flour, set it near the fire—When light, use it for your dough. Yeast cakes will keep good five or six months. They are very convenient to use in summer, as common yeast is so apt to ferment.

145. *Butter Biscuit.*

Melt a tea-cup of butter—mix it with two-thirds of a pint of milk, (if you have not any milk, water may be substituted, but the biscuit will not be as nice.) Put in a tea-spoonful of salt, half a tea-cup of yeast, (milk yeast is the best, see directions for making it)—stir in flour till it is stiff enough to mould up. A couple of eggs improve the biscuit, but are not essential. Set the dough in a warm place when risen, mould the dough with the hand into small cakes, lay them on flat tins that have been buttered. Let them remain half an hour before they are baked.

146. *Butter-milk Biscuit.*

Dissolve a couple of tea-spoonsful of saleratus in a tea-cup of sour milk—mix it with a pint of butter-milk, and a couple of tea-spoonsful of salt. Stir in flour until stiff enough to mould up. Mould it up into small cakes, and bake them immediately.

147. *Hard Biscuit.*

Weigh out four pounds of flour, and rub three pounds and a half of it with four ounces of butter, four beaten eggs, and a couple of tea-spoonsful of salt. Moisten it with milk, pound it out thin with a rolling-pin, sprinkle a little of the reserved flour over it lightly—roll it up and pound it out again, sprinkle on more of the flour—this operation continue to repeat till you get in all the reserved flour—then roll it out thin, cut it into cakes with a tumbler, lay them on flat buttered tins, cover them with a damp cloth, to prevent their drying. Bake them in a quick oven.

148. *Saleratus Biscuit.*

Put a couple of tea-spoonsful of saleratus in a pint of sour milk. If you have not any sour milk, put a table-spoonful of vinegar to a pint of sweet milk, set it in a warm place—as soon as it curdles, mix it with the saleratus—put in a couple of table-spoonfuls of melted butter, and flour to make them sufficiently stiff to roll out. Mould them up into small biscuit, and bake them immediately.

149. *Potato Biscuit.*

Boil mealy potatoes very soft, peel and mash them. To four good-sized potatoes, put a piece of butter, of the size of a hen's egg, a tea-spoonful of salt. When the butter has melted, put in half a pint of cold milk. If the milk cools the potatoes, put in a quarter of a pint of yeast, and flour to make them of the right consistency to mould up. Set them in a warm place—when risen, mould them up with the hand—let them remain ten or fifteen minutes before baking them.

150. *Sponge Biscuit.*

Stir into a pint of lukewarm milk half a tea-cup of melted butter, a tea-spoonful of salt, half a tea-cup of family, or a table-spoonful of brewers' yeast, (the latter is the best;) add flour till it is a very stiff batter. When light, drop this mixture by the large spoonful on to flat, buttered tins, several inches apart. Let them remain a few minutes before baking. Bake them in a quick oven till they are a light brown.

151. *Crackers.*

Rub six ounces of butter with two pounds of flour—dissolve a couple of tea-spoonsful of saleratus in a wine glass of milk, and strain it on to the flour—add a tea-spoonful of salt, and milk enough to enable you to roll it out. Beat it with a rolling-pin for half an hour, pounding it out thin—cut it into cakes with a tumbler—bake them about fifteen minutes, then take them from the oven. When the rest of your things are baked sufficiently, take them out, set in the crackers, and let them remain till baked hard and crispy.

152. *Cream Cakes.*

Mix half a pint of thick cream with the same quantity of milk, four eggs, and flour to render them just stiff enough to drop on buttered tins. They should be dropped by the large spoonful several inches apart, and baked in a quick oven.

153. *Crumpets.*

Take three tea-cups of raised dough, and work into it, with the hand, half a tea-cup of melted butter, three eggs, and milk to render it a thick batter. Turn it into a buttered bake pan—let it remain fifteen minutes, then put on a bake pan, heated so as to scorch flour. It will bake in half an hour.

154. *Rice Cakes.*

Mix a pint of rice boiled soft with a pint of milk, a tea-spoonful of salt, and three eggs, beaten to a froth. Stir in rice or wheat flour till of the right consistency to fry. If you like them baked, add two more eggs, and enough more flour to make them stiff enough to roll out, and cut them into cakes.

155. *Rice Ruffs.*

To a pint of rice flour put boiling water or milk sufficient to make a thick batter. Beat four eggs, (when it is cool,) and put in, together with a tea-spoonful of salt. Drop this mixture by the large spoonful into hot fat.

156. *Buckwheat Cakes.*

Mix a quart of buckwheat flour with a pint of lukewarm milk, (water will do, but is not as good,) and a tea-cup of yeast—set it in a warm place to rise. When light, (which will be in the course of eight or ten hours if family yeast is used, if brewers' yeast is used, they will rise much quicker,) add a tea-spoonful of salt—if sour, the same quantity of saleratus, dissolved in a little milk, and strained. If they are too thick, thin them with cold milk or water. Fry them in just fat enough to prevent their sticking to the frying pan.

157. *Economy Cakes.*

Rusked bread, or that which is old and sour, can be made into nice cakes. The bread should be cut into small pieces, and soaked in cold water till very soft. Then drain off the water, mash the bread fine—to three pints of the bread pulp put a couple of beaten eggs, three or four table-spoonsful of flour, and a little salt—dissolve a tea-spoonful of saleratus to a tea-cup of milk, strain it, then stir it into the bread—add more milk till it is of the right consistency to fry. The batter should be rather thicker than that of buckwheat cakes, and cooked in the same manner. Another way of making them, which is very good, is to mix half a pint of wheat flour with enough cold milk or water to render it a thick batter, and a couple of table-spoonsful of yeast. When light, mix the batter with the bread, (which should be previously soaked soft, and mashed fine,) add salt, and a tea-spoonful of saleratus, dissolved in a little milk. Fry them in just fat enough to prevent their sticking to the frying pan.

158. *Green Corn Cake.*

Mix a pint of grated green corn with three table-spoonsful of milk, a tea-cup of flour, half a tea-cup of melted butter, one egg, a tea-spoonful of salt, and half a tea-spoonful of pepper. Drop this mixture into hot butter by the spoonful, let the cakes fry eight or ten minutes. These cakes are nice served up with meat for dinner.

159. *Indian Corn Cake.*

Stir into a quart of sour or butter-milk a couple of tea-spoonsful of saleratus, a little salt, and sifted Indian meal to render it a thick batter—a little cream improves the cake—bake it in deep cake pans about an hour. When sour milk cannot be procured, boil sweet milk, and turn it on to the

Indian meal—when cool, put in three beaten eggs to a quart of the meal—add salt to the taste.

160. *Indian Slap Jacks.*

Scald a quart of Indian meal—when lukewarm, turn, stir in half a pint of flour, half a tea-cup of yeast, and a little salt. When light, fry them in just fat enough to prevent their sticking to the frying pan. Another method of making them, which is very nice, is to turn boiling milk or water on to the Indian meal, in the proportion of a quart of the former to a pint of the latter—stir in three table-spoonsful of flour, three eggs well beaten, and a couple of tea-spoonsful of salt.

161. *Journey or Johnny Cakes.*

Scald a quart of sifted Indian meal with sufficient water to make it a very thick batter. Stir in two or three tea-spoonsful of salt—mould it with the hand into small cakes. In order to mould them up, it will be necessary to rub a good deal of flour on the hands, to prevent their sticking. Fry them in nearly fat enough to cover them. When brown on the under side, they should be turned. It takes about twenty minutes to cook them. When cooked, split and butter them. Another way of making them, which is nice, is to scald the Indian meal, and put in saleratus, dissolved in milk and salt, in the proportion of a tea-spoonful of each to a quart of meal. Add two or three table-spoonsful of wheat flour, and drop the batter by the large spoonful into a frying pan. The batter should be of a very thick consistency, and there should be just fat enough in the frying pan to prevent the cakes sticking to it.

162. *Hoe Cakes.*

Scald a quart of Indian meal with just water enough to make a thick batter. Stir in a couple of tea-spoonsful of salt, and two table-spoonful of butter. Turn it into a buttered bake pan, and bake it half an hour.

163. *Muffins.*

Mix a quart of wheat flour smoothly with a pint and a half of lukewarm milk, half a tea-cup of yeast, a couple of beaten eggs, a heaping tea-spoonful of salt, and a couple of table-spoonful of lukewarm melted butter. Set the batter in a warm place to rise. When light, butter your muffin cups, turn in the mixture, and bake the muffins till a light brown.

164. *Raised Flour Waffles.*

Stir into a quart of flour sufficient lukewarm milk to make a thick batter. The milk should be stirred in gradually, so as to have it free from lumps. Put in a table-spoonful of melted butter, a couple of beaten eggs, a tea-spoonful of salt, and half a tea-cup of yeast. When risen, fill your waffle-irons with the batter, bake them on a hot bed of coals. When they have been on the fire between two and three minutes, turn the waffle-irons over—when brown on both sides, they are sufficiently baked. The waffle-irons should be well greased with lard, and very hot, before each one is put in. The waffles should be buttered as soon as cooked. Serve them up with powdered white sugar and cinnamon.

165. *Quick Waffles.*

Mix flour and cold milk together, to make a thick batter. To a quart of the flour put six beaten eggs, a table-spoonful of melted butter, and a tea-spoonful of salt. Some cooks add a quarter of a pound of sugar, and half a nutmeg. Bake them immediately.

166. *Rice Waffles.*

Take a tea-cup and a half of boiled rice—warm it with a pint of milk, mix it smooth, then take it from the fire, stir in a pint of cold milk, and a tea-spoonful of salt. Beat four eggs, and stir them in, together with sufficient flour to make a thick batter.

167. *Rice Wafers.*

Melt a quarter of a pound of butter, and mix it with a pound of rice flour, a tea-spoonful of salt, and a wine glass of wine. Beat four eggs, and stir in, together with just cold milk enough to enable you to roll them out easily. They should be rolled out as thin as possible, cut with a wine glass into cakes, and baked in a moderate oven, on buttered flat tins.

168. *Rules to be observed in making nice Cake.*

Cake, to be good, must be made of nice materials. The butter, eggs, and flour, should not be stale, and the sugar should be of a light color, and dry. Brown sugar answers very well for most kinds of cake, if rolled free from lumps, and stirred to a cream with the butter. The flour should be sifted, and if damp, dried perfectly, otherwise it will make the cake heavy. The eggs should be beaten to a froth; and the cake will be more delicate if the yelks and whites are beaten separately. Saleratus and soda should be perfectly dissolved, and strained before they are stirred into the cake. Raisins for cake should have the seeds taken out. Zante currants should be rinsed in several waters to cleanse them, rubbed in a dry cloth to get out the sticks, and then spread on platters, and dried perfectly, before they are put into the cake. Almonds should be blanched, which is done by turning boiling water on them, and letting them remain in it till the skins will rub off easily. When blanched, dry them, then pound them fine, with rosewater, to prevent their oiling. When the weather is cold, the materials for cake should be moderately warmed, before mixing them together. All kinds of cake that are made without yeast are better for being stirred, till just before they are baked. The butter and sugar should be stirred together till white, then the eggs, flour, and spice, added. Saleratus and cream should not be put in till just before the cake is baked—add the fruit last. Butter the cake pans well. The cake will be less liable to burn if the pans are lined with white buttered paper. The cake should not be moved while baking if it can be avoided, as moving it is apt to make it heavy. The quicker most kinds of cake are baked, the lighter and better they will be; but the oven should not be of such a furious heat as to burn them. It is impossible to give any exact rules as to the time to be allowed for baking various kinds of cake, as so much depends on the heat of the oven. It should be narrowly watched while in the oven, and if it browns too fast, it should be covered with a thick paper. To ascertain when rich cake is sufficiently baked, stick a clean broom splinter through the thickest part of the loaf—if none of the cake adheres to the splinter, it is sufficiently baked. When cake that is baked on flat tins moves easily on them, it is sufficiently baked.

169. *Frosting for Cake.*

Allow for the white of one egg nine heaping tea-spoonsful of double refined sugar, and one of nice Poland starch. The sugar and starch should be pounded, and sifted through a very fine sieve. Beat the whites of eggs to a stiff froth, so that you can turn the plate upside down, without the eggs falling from it—then stir in the sugar gradually, with a wooden spoon—stir it ten or fifteen minutes without any cessation—then add a tea-spoonful of lemon juice, (vinegar will answer, but is not as nice)—put in sufficient rosewater to flavor it. If you wish to color it pink, stir in a few grains of cochineal powder, or rose pink—if you wish to have it of a blue tinge, add a little of what is called the powder blue. Lay the frosting on the cake with a knife, soon after it is taken from the oven—smooth it over, and let it remain in a cool place till hard. To frost a common sized loaf of cake, allow the white of one egg, and half of another.

170. *Sponge Gingerbread.*

Melt a piece of butter of the size of a hen's egg—mix it with a pint of nice molasses, a table-spoonful of ginger, and a quart of flour. Dissolve a heaping table-spoonful of saleratus in half a pint of milk, strain and mix it with the rest of the ingredients, add sufficient flour to enable you to roll it out easily, roll it out about half an inch thick, and bake it on flat tins in a quick oven. Gingerbread made in this manner will be light and spongy if baked quick, and made of nice molasses, but it will not keep good so long as hard gingerbread.

171. *Hard Molasses Gingerbread.*

To a pint of molasses put half a tea-cup of melted butter, a table-spoonful of ginger, and a quart of flour. Dissolve a tea-spoonful of saleratus in half a pint of water, and stir it in, together with flour sufficient to enable you to roll it out. Bake it in a moderately warm oven.

172. *Soft Molasses Gingerbread.*

Melt a tea-cup of butter—mix it with a pint of molasses, a table-spoonful of ginger, a pint of flour, and a couple of beaten eggs. Fresh lemon peel, cut into small strips, improves it. Dissolve a couple of tea-spoonsful of saleratus in half a pint of milk, and stir it into the cake. Add flour to render it of the consistency of unbaked pound cake. Bake it in deep pans about half an hour.

173. *Sugar Gingerbread.*

Mix a pound of sugar with six ounces of butter. Beat four eggs, and stir them into the butter and sugar, together with three tea-spoonsful of ginger. Stir in gradually a pound and a half of flour—dissolve a tea-spoonful of saleratus in a wine glass of milk, and stir it in, and bake the gingerbread immediately.

174. *Ginger Snaps.*

Melt a quarter of a pound of butter, the same quantity of lard—mix them with a quarter of a pound of brown sugar, a pint of molasses, a couple of table-spoonsful of ginger, and a quart of flour. Dissolve a couple of tea-spoonsful of saleratus in a wine glass of milk, and strain it into the cake—add sufficient flour to enable you to roll it out very thin, cut it into small cakes, and bake them in a slow oven.

175. *Spice Cakes.*

Melt a tea-cup of butter, mix it with a tea-cup of sugar, and half a tea-cup of molasses. Stir in a tea-spoonful of cinnamon, the same quantity of ginger, a grated nutmeg, and a tea-spoonful each of caraway and coriander seed—put in a tea-spoonful of saleratus, dissolved in half a tea-cup of water, stir in flour till stiff enough to roll out thin, cut it into cakes, and bake them in a slow oven.

176. *Cider Cake.*

Stir together a tea-cup of butter, three of sugar—beat four eggs, and put into the cake, together with two tea-cups of flour, and a grated nutmeg. Dissolve a tea-spoonful of saleratus in half a tea-cup of milk, strain it, and mix it with the above ingredients—stir in a tea-cup of cider, and four more cups of flour.

177. *Bannock or Indian Meal Cakes.*

Stir to a cream a pound and a quarter of brown sugar, a pound of butter—beat six eggs, and mix them with the sugar and butter—add a tea-spoonful of cinnamon or ginger—stir in a pound and three quarters of white Indian meal, and a quarter of a pound of wheat flour, (the meal should be sifted.) Bake it in small cups, and let it remain in them till cold.

178. *Rich Cookies.*

Rub together, till white, a tea-cup of butter, two of sugar—then stir in a couple of beaten eggs, a little flour, grate in a nutmeg—dissolve a tea-spoonful of saleratus in a tea-cup of milk or water, strain it on to the cake, then add flour till stiff enough to roll out easily. If you cannot roll out the cake without its sticking to the board and rolling-pin, (which should be previously floured,) work in more flour, stamp and cut it into cakes—bake them in a moderately warm oven.

179. *Plain Tea Cakes.*

Mix thoroughly a tea-cup and a half of sugar, half a tea-cup of butter, stir in a little flour, and half a nutmeg. Dissolve a tea-spoonful of saleratus in a tea-cup of milk, strain and mix it with the cake—add flour till stiff enough to roll out—roll it out half an inch thick, cut it into cakes, bake them on flat buttered tins, in a quick oven. If baked slow, they will not be good.

180. *New Year's Cookies.*

Weigh out a pound of sugar, three-quarters of a pound of butter—stir them to a cream, then add three beaten eggs, a grated nutmeg, two table-spoonsful of caraway seed, and a pint of flour. Dissolve a tea-spoonful of saleratus in a tea-cup of milk, strain and mix it with half a tea-cup of cider, and stir it into the cookies—then add flour to make them sufficiently stiff to roll out. Bake them as soon as cut into cakes, in a quick oven, till a light brown.

181. *Shrewsbury Cake.*

Stir together three-quarters of a pound of sugar, half a pound of butter. When white, add five beaten eggs, a tea-spoonful of rosewater, or a nutmeg, and a pound of flour. Drop it with a large spoon on to flat tins that have been buttered—sift sugar over them.

182. *Tunbridge Cake.*

Six ounces of butter, the same quantity of sugar, three-quarters of a pound of flour, a couple of eggs, and a tea-spoonful of rosewater. Stir to a cream the butter and sugar, then add the eggs, flour, and spice. Roll it out thin, and cut it into small cakes.

183. *Jumbles.*

Stir together, till of a light color, a pound of sugar, and half the weight of butter—then add eight eggs, beaten to a froth, essence of lemon, or rosewater, to the taste, and flour to make them sufficiently stiff to roll out. Roll them out in powdered sugar, about half an inch thick, cut it into strips about half an inch wide, and four inches long, join the ends together, so as to form rings—lay them on flat tins that have been buttered—bake them in a quick oven.

184. *Composition Cake.*

Five tea-cups of flour, three of sugar, two of butter, five eggs, a tea-spoonful of saleratus, a tea-cup of milk, a wine glass of wine, or brandy, one nutmeg, a pound of raisins. Stir the sugar and butter to a cream, then add the eggs, beaten to a froth, and part of the flour and the spice—dissolve the saleratus in the milk, strain and mix it with the brandy, stir it into the cake, with the rest of the flour—add the raisins just before the cake is put into the pans.

185. *Rusk.*

Melt half a pound of butter, and mix it with two-thirds of a pint of milk—flour to make a thick batter. Add three table-spoonsful of yeast, and set the batter in a warm place to rise. When light, beat two eggs, with half a pound of rolled sugar—work it into the batter with the hand, add a tea-spoonful of salt, a tea-spoonful of cinnamon, and flour to make them sufficiently stiff to mould up. Mould them up into cakes of the size you would make biscuit, lay them on flat tins, previously buttered, let them remain till of a spongy lightness, before baking. They will bake, in a quick oven, in the course of fifteen minutes.

186. *Whigs.*

Mix half a pound of sugar with six ounces of butter, a couple of beaten eggs, a tea-spoonful of cinnamon. Stir in two pounds of flour, a tea-cup of yeast, and milk sufficient to make a thick batter. When light, bake them in small cups.

187. *Nut Cakes.*

Heat a pint of milk just lukewarm—stir into it a tea-cup of lard, (the lard should be melted.) Stir in flour, till it is a thick batter, then add a small tea-cup of yeast. Set it in a warm place—when light, work in two tea-cups and a half of rolled sugar, four eggs beaten to a froth, two tea-spoonsful of cinnamon, and one of salt. Knead in flour to make it sufficiently stiff to roll out—keep it in a warm place, till risen again. When it appears of a spongy lightness, roll it out about half an inch thick, cut it into cakes with a wine glass, let them remain fifteen or twenty minutes before boiling them—boil them in a pot, with about a couple of pounds of lard. The fat should be hot enough to boil up as they are put in, and a brisk fire kept under the pot. It should be shaken constantly while they are boiling. Only a few should be boiled at once—if crowded, they will not fry well. If you wish to have them look nice, dip them into powdered white sugar as soon as fried. The same lard, with a little more added, will answer to fry several batches of cakes in, if not burnt.

188. *Crollers.*

Dissolve a tea-spoonful of saleratus in four table-spoonsful of milk, or leave out one spoonful of milk, and substitute one of wine. Strain it on to half a pint of flour, four table-spoonsful of melted butter, or lard, and a tea-spoonful of salt. Beat four eggs, with six heaping table-spoonsful of rolled sugar—work them into the rest of the ingredients, together with a grated nutmeg—add flour to make them stiff enough to roll out easily. They should be rolled out about half an inch thick, cut with a jagging iron or knife into strips about half an inch wide, and twisted, so as to form small cakes. Heat a pound of lard in a deep pot or kettle, (some cooks use a frying pan to fry crollers in, but they are more apt to burn when fried in a pan.) The fat should boil up, as the cakes are laid in, and they should be constantly watched while frying. When brown on the under side, turn them —when brown on both sides, they are sufficiently cooked.

189. *Molasses Dough Cake.*

Melt half a tea-cup of butter, mix it with a tea-cup of molasses, the juice and chopped rind of a fresh lemon, a tea-spoonful of cinnamon—work the whole with the hand into three tea-cups of raised dough, together with a couple of beaten eggs. Work it with the hand for ten or twelve minutes, then put it into buttered pans. Let it remain ten or fifteen minutes before baking it.

190. *Sugar Dough Cake.*

Dissolve a tea-spoonful of saleratus in a wine glass of wine, or milk—strain it on to three tea-cups of raised dough. Work into the dough a tea-cup of lukewarm melted butter, two tea-cups of rolled sugar, three eggs well beaten, and a couple of tea-spoonsful of cinnamon. Work the whole well together for a quarter of an hour, then put it into cake pans. Let it stand in a warm place fifteen or twenty minutes, before baking it.

191. *Measure Cake.*

Stir to a cream a tea-cup of butter, two of sugar, then stir in four eggs beaten to a froth, a grated nutmeg, and a pint of flour. Stir it until just before it is baked. It is good either baked in cups or pans.

192. *French Cake.*

One pound of sugar, three quarters of a pound of butter, a pound and a half of flour, twelve eggs, a gill each of wine, brandy, and of milk. Mix the sugar and butter together—when white, add the eggs, beaten to a froth, (the whites and yelks should be separated)—then stir in the flour, the milk and wine, and one-fourth of a grated nutmeg. Just before it is baked, add three-quarters of a pound of seeded raisins, a quarter of a pound of citron, and a quarter of a pound of almonds, blanched and pounded fine. To blanch almonds, see directions in No. 168.

193. *Washington Cake.*

Stir together, till quite white, a pound of sugar, three-quarters of a pound of butter, then add four beaten eggs. Stir in gradually a pound and a half of flour. Dissolve a tea-spoonful of saleratus in a tea-cup of milk, strain and mix it with a glass of wine, then stir it into the cake, together with a tea-spoonful of rosewater, and half a nutmeg. Just before it is baked, add a pound of seeded raisins.

194. *Cup Cake.*

Mix three tea-cups of sugar with one and a half of butter. When white, beat three eggs, and stir them into the butter and sugar, together with three tea-cups of sifted flour, and rosewater or essence of lemon to the taste. Dissolve a tea-spoonful of saleratus in a tea-cup of milk, strain it into the cake, then add three more tea-cups of sifted flour. Bake the cake immediately, either in cups or pans.

195. *Plain Cream Cake.*

Dissolve a tea-spoonful of saleratus in a wine glass of milk, strain it on to a little sifted flour, beat three eggs with a tea-cup of rolled sugar, mix them with the above ingredients, together with half a grated nutmeg. Add a tea-cup of thick cream, and sifted flour to render it of the consistency of unbaked pound cake. Bake it as soon as the cream and flour are well mixed in, as stirring the cream much decomposes it.

196. *Rich Cream Cake.*

Stir together, till very white, half a pound of butter, three-quarters of a pound of sugar. Beat the whites and yelks of seven eggs separately to a froth, stir them into the cake—put in a wine glass of brandy, a grated nutmeg, and a pound and a half of sifted flour. Just before it is baked, add half a pint of thick cream, and a pound of seeded raisins.

197. *Cymbals.*

Half a pound of sugar, a quarter of a pound of butter, a couple of eggs, half a nutmeg, a tea-spoonful of saleratus, half a tea-cup of milk. Stir the butter and sugar together, then add the eggs and a little flour, stir in the milk and saleratus, which should be previously strained, then add enough flour to make it stiff enough to roll out—roll it out half an inch thick, in pounded white sugar, cut it with a tumbler into cakes, and bake them on flat buttered tins.

198. *Rich Loaf Cake.*

Stir gradually into a pint of lukewarm milk a pound of sifted wheat flour, add a small tea-cup of yeast, and set it where it will rise quick. When of a spongy lightness, weigh out a pound of butter, a pound and a quarter of nice sugar—stir them to a cream, then work them with the hand into the sponge. Beat four eggs to a froth, the whites and yelks separately—mix the eggs with the cake, together with a wine glass of wine, one of brandy, a quarter of an ounce of mace, or one nutmeg. Cinnamon is good spice for loaf cake, but it turns it a dark color. Add another pound of flour, and work it with the hand for fifteen or twenty minutes. (The longer it is worked, the more delicate will be the cake.) Let it remain till risen again—when perfectly light, beat it a few minutes with the hand, then add a couple of pounds of seeded raisins, a quarter of a pound of citron, or almonds blanched, and pounded fine. Butter three common sized cake pans, and put the cake into them—let them remain half an hour in a warm place, before setting them in the oven. Bake the cake in a quick, but not a furious oven, from an hour and fifteen to thirty minutes, according to the heat of the oven. If it browns too fast, cover it, while baking, with thick paper.

199. *Plain Loaf Cake.*

Mix together a pint of lukewarm milk, two quarts of sifted flour, a small tea-cup of yeast. Set the batter where it will rise quick. When perfectly light, work in with the hand four beaten eggs, a tea-spoonful of salt, two of cinnamon, a wine glass of brandy or wine. Stir a pound of sugar with three-quarters of a pound of butter—when white, work it into the cake, add another quart of sifted flour, and beat the whole well with the hand ten or fifteen minutes, then set it where it will rise again. When of a spongy lightness, put it into buttered cake pans, and let them stand fifteen or twenty minutes before baking. Add if you like a pound and a half of raisins, just before putting the cake into the pans.

200. *Shelah, or Quick Loaf Cake.*

Melt half a pound of butter—when cool, work it into a pound and a half of raised dough. Beat four eggs with three-quarters of a pound of rolled sugar, mix it with the dough, together with a wine glass of wine, or brandy, a tea-spoonful of cinnamon, and a grated nutmeg. Dissolve a tea-spoonful of saleratus in a small tea-cup of milk, strain it on to the dough, work the whole well together for a quarter of an hour, then add a pound of seeded raisins, and put it into cake pans. Let them remain twenty minutes before setting them in the oven.

201. *Rice Cake.*

Mix ten ounces of ground rice, three of wheat flour, eight ounces of powdered white sugar. Sift the whole by degrees into the beaten yelks of eight eggs. Add the whites of the eggs, beaten to a stiff froth, and half a grated nutmeg. Bake the cake in deep pans as soon as the ingredients are well mixed in. The cake will bake sufficiently in the course of twenty minutes, if the oven is hot.

202. *Diet Bread.*

Sift a pound of flour, mix it with a pound of rolled sugar. Beat eight eggs to a froth, and stir the flour and sugar in very gradually. Season it to the taste with essence of lemon or rosewater. Bake it from fifteen to twenty minutes.

203. *Lemon Cake.*

Stir together, till very white, a pound of sugar, half a pound of butter—then add eight eggs, beaten to a froth, (the whites and yelks should be beaten separately,) the grated rind of two lemons, and the juice of half a lemon. Stir in gradually a pound of sifted flour. Line a couple of cake pans with white buttered paper, turn the cake into them, and bake it in a quick oven.

204. *Scotch Cake.*

Stir to a cream a pound of sugar, and three-quarters of a pound of butter—put in the juice and grated rind of a lemon, a wine glass of brandy. Separate the whites and yelks of nine eggs, beat them to a froth, and stir them into the cake—then add a pound of sifted flour, and just before it is put in the cake pans, a pound of seeded raisins.

205. *Pound Cake.*

Mix a pound of sugar with three-quarters of a pound of butter. When worked white, stir in the yelks of eight eggs, beaten to a froth, then the whites. Add a pound of sifted flour, and mace or nutmeg to the taste. If you wish to have your cake particularly nice, stir in, just before you put it into the pans, a quarter of a pound of citron, or almonds blanched, and powdered fine in rosewater.

206. *Confectioner's Pound Cake.*

Stir together a pound and a quarter of sugar, three quarters of a pound of butter. When of a light color, stir in twelve beaten eggs, a pound and a half of sifted flour, and mace or nutmeg to the taste.

207. *Queen's Cake.*

Rub together, till very white, a pound of sugar, three quarters of a pound of butter. Mix a wine glass of wine, one of brandy, one of milk, and if you wish to have the cake look dark, put in a tea-spoonful of saleratus. Stir them into the butter and sugar, together with a pound of flour, a tea-spoonful of rosewater, or essence of lemon, a quarter of an ounce of mace. Beat the whites and yelks separately of six eggs—if no saleratus is used, two more eggs will be necessary. When beaten to a froth, mix them with the cake. Stir the whole well together, then add, just before baking it, half a pound of seeded raisins, the same weight of Zante currants, a quarter of a pound of citron, or almonds blanched, and pounded fine in rosewater. The fruit should be stirred in gradually, a handful of each alternately. Line a couple of three pint tin pans with buttered white paper, put in the cake, and bake it directly. If it browns too fast, cover it with paper. It takes from an hour and a quarter to an hour and a half to bake it, according to the heat of the oven.

208. *Delicate Cake.*

Stir to a cream a pound of powdered white sugar, seven ounces of butter —then add the whites of sixteen eggs, beaten to a stiff froth, half a nutmeg, or a tea-spoonful of rosewater. Stir in gradually a pound of sifted flour, and bake the cake immediately. The yelks of the eggs can be used for custards.

209. *Jelly Cake.*

Rub together, till white, half a pound of sugar, six ounces of butter. Beat eight eggs to a froth, and stir into the butter and sugar, together with a pound of sifted flour. Add the juice and grated rind of a fresh lemon, and turn this mixture on to scolloped tin plates, that have been well buttered. The cake should not be more than a quarter of an inch thick on each of the plates. Bake them directly, in a quick oven, till a light brown. Pile them on a plate with a layer of jelly or marmalade between each of the cakes, and a layer on the top.

210. *Strawberry Cake.*

Mix a quart of flour with a tea-spoonful of salt, four beaten eggs, and a tea-cup of thick cream, or melted butter. Add sufficient milk to enable you to roll it out—roll it out thin, line a shallow cake pan with part of it, then put in a thick layer of nice ripe strawberries, strew on sufficient white sugar to sweeten the strawberries, cover them with a thin layer of the crust, then add another layer of strawberries and sugar—cover the whole with another layer of crust, and bake it in a quick oven about twenty-five minutes.

211. *Superior Sponge Cake.*

Take the weight of ten eggs in powdered loaf sugar, beat it to a froth with the yelks of twelve eggs, put in the grated rind of a fresh lemon, leaving out the white part—add half the juice. Beat the whites of twelve eggs to a stiff froth, and mix them with the sugar and butter. Stir the whole without any cessation for fifteen minutes, then stir in gradually the weight of six eggs in sifted flour. As soon as the flour is well mixed in, turn the cake into pans lined with buttered paper—bake it immediately in a quick, but not a furiously hot oven. It will bake in the course of twenty minutes. If it bakes too fast, cover it with thick paper.

212. *Good Sponge Cake.*

Beat together the yelks of ten eggs, with a pound of powdered white sugar—beat to a stiff froth the whites of the eggs, and stir them into the yelks and sugar. Beat the whole ten or fifteen minutes, then stir in gradually three-quarters of a pound of sifted flour. Flavor it with a nutmeg, or the grated rind of a lemon. Bake it as soon as the flour and spices are well mixed in.

213. *Almond Cake.*

Beat the yelks of twelve eggs to a froth, with a pound of powdered white sugar. Beat the whites of nine eggs to a stiff froth, and stir them into the yelks and sugar. When the whole has been stirred together for ten minutes, add gradually a pound of sifted flour, and half a pound of almonds, blanched and pounded fine, then stir in three table-spoonsful of thick cream. As soon as the ingredients are well mixed in, turn the cake into buttered pans, and bake it immediately. Frost the cake with the reserved whites of the eggs as soon as it is baked.

214. *Fruit Cake.*

One pound of flour, one of sugar, three-quarters of a pound of butter, two pounds of seeded raisins, two of currants, one of citron, a quarter of a pound of almonds, half an ounce of mace, a tea-spoonful of rosewater, a wine glass of brandy, one of wine, and ten eggs. Stir the sugar and butter to a cream, then add the whites and yelks of the eggs, beaten separately to a froth—stir in the flour gradually, then the wine, brandy, and spice. Add the fruit just before it is put into the pans. It takes over two hours to bake it if the loaves are thick—if the loaves are thin, it will bake in less time. This kind of cake is the best after it has been made three or four weeks, and it will keep good five or six months.

215. *Black Cake.*

One pound of flour, one of sugar, fourteen ounces of butter, ten eggs, three pounds of seeded raisins, three pounds of Zante currants, and one pound of citron, a wine glass of wine, one of brandy, and one of milk, a tea-spoonful of saleratus, a table-spoonful of molasses, a table-spoonful of cinnamon, a tea-spoonful of cloves, a quarter of an ounce of mace, or one nutmeg. The sugar should be the brown kind, and stirred a few minutes with the butter, then the eggs beaten to a froth, and stirred in. Brown the flour in a pan, over a few coals—stir it constantly to prevent its burning. It should be done before you commence making the cake, so as to have it get cold. Stir it into the butter and sugar gradually, then add the molasses and spice. Dissolve the saleratus in the milk, then strain it, and mix it with the brandy and wine, to curdle them—stir the whole into the cake. Just before you put it into the cake pans, stir in the fruit gradually, a handful of each alternately.

When well mixed in, put it into cake pans, and bake it immediately. If baked in thick loaves, it takes from two hours and a half to three hours to bake it sufficiently. The oven should not be of a furious heat. Black cake cuts the best when three or four weeks old.

216. *Maccaroons.*

Soak half a pound of sweet almonds in boiling hot water, till the skins will rub off easily—wipe them dry. When you have rubbed off the skins, pound them fine with rosewater. Beat the whites of three eggs to a stiff froth, then stir in gradually half a pound of powdered white sugar, then add the almonds. When the almonds are well mixed in, drop the mixture in small parcels on buttered baking plates, several inches apart, sift sugar over them, and bake them in a slow oven.

217. *Cocoanut Cakes.*

Take equal weights of grated cocoanut and powdered white sugar, (the brown part of the cocoanut should be cut off before grating it)—add the whites of eggs beaten to a stiff froth, in the proportion of half a dozen to a pound each of cocoanut and sugar. There should be just eggs enough to wet up the whole stiff. Drop the mixture on to buttered plates, in parcels of the size of a cent, several inches apart. Bake them immediately in a moderately warm oven.

218. *Tory Wafers.*

Melt a tea-cup of butter, half a one of lard, and mix them with a quart of flour, a couple of beaten eggs, a tea-spoonful of salt, a wine glass of wine. Add milk till of the right consistency to roll out—roll it out about the third of an inch in thickness, cut it into cakes with a wine glass, lay them on buttered baking plates, and bake them a few minutes. Frost them as soon as baked, and sprinkle comfits or sugar sand on the top.

219. *Sugar Drops.*

Stir to a cream three ounces of butter, six of powdered white sugar—then add three beaten eggs, half a pound of sifted flour, half of a nutmeg. Drop this mixture by the large spoonful on to buttered plates, several inches apart, sprinkle small sugar plums on the top, and bake them directly.

220. *Savoy Cakes.*

Beat eight eggs to a froth—the whites and yelks should be beaten separately, then mixed together, and a pound of powdered white sugar stirred in gradually. Beat the whole well together, for eight or ten minutes, then add the grated rind of a fresh lemon, and half the juice, a pound of sifted flour, a couple of table-spoonsful of coriander seed. Drop this mixture by the large spoonful on to buttered baking plates, several inches apart, sift white sugar over them, and bake them immediately in a quick, but not a furiously hot oven.

221. *Almond Cheese Cakes.*

Boil a pint of new milk—beat three eggs, and stir into the milk while boiling. When it boils up, take it from the fire, put in half a wine glass of wine, separate the curd from the whey, and put to the curd three eggs, six ounces of powdered white sugar, previously beaten together. Add a tea-spoonful of rosewater, half a pound of sweet almonds that have been blanched and pounded fine, a quarter of a pound of melted butter. Mix the whole well together, then pour it into small pans that are lined with pastry. Ornament the top with Zante currants, and almonds cut in thin slips—bake them directly.

222. *Flummery.*

Lay sponge or Savoy cakes in a deep dish—pour on white wine sufficient to make them quite moist. Make a rich boiled custard, using only the yelks of the eggs—turn it over the cakes when cool—beat the whites of the eggs to a froth, and turn them over the whole.

223. *Floating Island.*

Mix a pint and a half of sweet thick cream with a gill of wine, the juice of half a lemon, and a tea-spoonful of essence of lemon, or rosewater. Sweeten the whole with powdered loaf sugar—turn it into a deep dish. Beat the whites of four eggs to a froth, and stir in half a pound of any dark-colored preserved small fruit you may happen to have. Beat the whole to a strong froth, then turn it into the centre of the cream.

224. *Whip Syllabub.*

Take good sweet cream—to each pint put six ounces of double refined, powdered white sugar, half a tumbler of white wine, the juice and grated rind of a lemon. Beat the whole well together—put jelly in glasses, and cover them with the froth as fast as it rises.

225. *Ornamental Froth for Blanc Mange or Creams.*

Beat the whites of four eggs to a froth, then stir in half a pound of preserved raspberries, cranberries, or strawberries—beat the whole well together, then turn it over the top of your creams or blanc mange.

226. *Ice Currants.*

Take large bunches of ripe currants, wash and drain them dry, then dip them into the whites of eggs, previously beaten to a stiff froth. Lay them on a sieve, at such a distance from each other as not to touch—sift double refined sugar over them thick, and set them in a warm place to dry.

227. *Apple Snow.*

Put a dozen good tart apples into cold water, set them over a slow fire. When soft, drain off the water, pull the skins from the apples, take out the cores, and lay the apples in a deep dish. Beat the whites of twelve eggs to a strong froth—put half a pound of powdered white sugar on the apples, beat them to a strong froth, then add the beaten eggs. Beat the whole to a stiff snow, then turn it into a dessert dish, and ornament it with myrtle or box.

228. *Comfits.*

Mix a pound of white sugar with just sufficient water to make a thick syrup. When the sugar has dissolved, drop in a pound of coriander seed, then drain off the syrup, and put the seeds in a sieve, with two or three ounces of flour—shake them well in it, then set them where they will dry. When dry, put them in the syrup again, repeat the above process till they are of the size you wish.

229. *Isinglass Blanc Mange.*

Pull an ounce of mild white isinglass into small pieces—rinse them, and put to them a quart of milk if the weather is hot, and three pints if it is cold weather. Set it on a few coals, stir it constantly till the isinglass dissolves, then sweeten it to the taste with double refined loaf sugar, put in a small stick of cinnamon, a vanilla bean, or blade of mace. Set it where it will boil five or six minutes, stirring it constantly. Strain it, and fill the moulds with it—let it remain in them till cold. The same bean will do to use several times.

230. *Calf's Feet Blanc Mange.*

Boil four feet in five quarts of water, without any salt. When the liquor is reduced to one quart, strain and mix it with one quart of milk, several sticks of cinnamon, or a vanilla bean. Boil the whole ten minutes, sweeten it to the taste with white sugar, strain it, and fill your moulds with it.

231. *Rice Flour Blanc Mange.*

Mix four table-spoonsful of ground rice, smoothly, with half a pint of cold milk, then stir it into a quart of boiling milk. Put in the grated rind of a lemon, and half the juice, a blade of mace—sweeten to the taste with white sugar. Boil the whole seven or eight minutes, stirring it frequently. Take it from the fire—when cool, put in the beaten whites of three eggs, put it back on the fire, stir it constantly till nearly boiling hot, then turn it into moulds, or deep cups, and let it remain till cold. This is nice food for invalids.

232. *Rice Blanc Mange.*

Boil a tea-cup of rice in a pint of water, with a blade of mace, and a tea-spoonful of salt. When it swells out and becomes dry, add sufficient milk to prevent its burning. Let it boil till quite soft, stirring it constantly to keep it from burning—sweeten it with white sugar. Dip your moulds in cold water, then turn in the rice, without drying the moulds. Let the rice remain in the moulds till it becomes quite cold. Turn it into dessert dishes, ornament it with marmalade cut in slices, and box and serve it up with cream or preserved strawberries. It should be made the day before it is to be eaten, in order to have it become firm.

233. *Snow Cream.*

Beat the whites of four eggs to a stiff froth—then stir in two table-spoonsful of powdered white sugar, a table-spoonful of sweet wine, a tea-spoonful of rosewater. Beat the whole together, then add a pint of thick cream. This is a nice accompaniment to a dessert of sweetmeats.

234. *Orange Cream.*

Beat the yelks of eight eggs, and the whites of two, to a froth, then stir in half a pound of powdered white sugar—add half a pint of wine, and the juice of six fresh oranges, and the juice of one lemon. Flavor it with orange-flower water—strain it, and set it on a few coals—stir it till it thickens, then add a piece of butter, of the size of a nutmeg. When the butter has melted, take it from the fire, continue to stir it till cool, then fill your glasses with it. Beat up the whites of the eggs to a froth, and lay the froth on top of the glasses of cream.

235. *Lemon Cream.*

Pare four fresh lemons very thin, so as to get none of the white part. Soak the rinds twelve hours in half a pint of cold water, then add the juice of the lemons, and half a pint more of cold water. Beat to a froth the whites of eight eggs, and the yelks of three—strain the lemon-juice and water, mix it with the eggs—set the whole on a few coals, sweeten it with double refined sugar, stir it till it grows thick, then take it from the fire, stir it till cold—serve it up in glasses.

236. Ice Creams.

Sweeten thick rich cream with powdered white sugar—it should be made very sweet, as the process of freezing extracts a great deal of the saccharine matter. Essence of lemon, the juice of strawberries or pine-apples, are nice to flavor the cream with—the juice should be sweetened before being mixed with the cream. Where cream cannot be procured, a custard, made in the following manner, may be substituted: To a quart of milk put the beaten yelks of four eggs, the rind of a lemon, or a vanilla bean—set it on a few coals, make it extremely sweet, with white sugar—stir it constantly till scalding hot—care must be taken that it does not boil. Take it from the fire, take out the bean, or lemon peel—when perfectly cold, put it in an ice cream form—if one cannot be procured, a milk kettle, with a tight cover, may be substituted. Set the form into the centre of a tub that is large enough to leave a space of five inches from the form to the outside of the tub. Fill the space round the form with alternate layers of finely cracked ice and rock salt, having a layer of ice last, and the whole should be just as high as the form. Care should be taken to keep the salt from the cream. The tub should be covered with a woollen cloth while the cream is freezing, and the form should be constantly shaken. If you wish to shape the cream, turn it into moulds as soon as it freezes, set them in the tub, let them remain till just before they are to be eaten, then dip them in warm water, and take them out instantly, and turn them into dessert dishes.

237. Pastry.

For a good common pie-crust allow half a pound of shortening to a pound of flour. If liked quite short, allow three-quarters of a pound of shortening to a pound of the flour. Pie crust looks the nicest made entirely of lard, but it does not taste so good as it does to have some butter used in making it. In winter, beef shortening, mixed with butter, makes good plain pie crust. Rub half of the shortening with two-thirds of the flour—to each pound of flour put a tea-spoonful of salt. When the shortening is thoroughly mixed with the flour, add just sufficient cold water to render it moist enough to roll out easily. Divide the crust into two equal portions—lay one of them one side for the upper crust, take the other, roll it out quite thin, flouring your rolling-board and pin, so that the crust will not stick to them, and line your pie plates, which should be previously buttered—fill your plates with your fruit, then roll out the upper crust as thin as possible, spread on the reserved shortening, sprinkle over the flour, roll it up, and cut it into as many pieces as you have pies to cover. Roll each one out about half an inch thick, and cover the pies—trim the edges off neatly with a knife, and press the crust down, round the edge of the plate, with a jagging iron, so that the juices of the fruit may not run out while baking. Pastry, to be nice, should be baked in a quick oven. In cold weather it is necessary to warm the shortening before using it for pie crust, but it must not be melted, or the crust will not be flaky.

238. *Puff Paste, or Confectioner's Pastry.*

Weigh out a pound and a quarter of sifted flour, and a pound of butter. Rub about one-third of the butter with two-thirds of the flour, a tea-spoonful of salt. When the butter is thoroughly mixed with the flour, add one beaten egg, and cold water to moisten it sufficiently to roll out. Sprinkle part of the reserved flour on a board, cut the butter into small pieces, and roll them out as thin as possible. In order to do so, it will be necessary to rub a great deal of the flour on the moulding-board and rolling-pin. Lay the butter, as fast as rolled out, on to a floured plate, each piece by itself—roll out the pastry as thin as it can be rolled, cover it with the rolled butter, sprinkle on part of the reserved flour, and roll the crust up. Continue to roll out the crust, and put on the reserved butter and flour, till the whole is used. Roll it out lightly, about half an inch thick, for the upper crust, or rim to your pies—plain pie crust should be used for the under crust to the pies. Puff pastry, to be nice, should be baked in a quick oven till of a light brown color. If it browns before the fruit in the pie is sufficiently baked, cover it with thick paper.

239. *Apple Pie.*

When apples are very small and green, they are nice stewed whole, with the skins on, and strained when soft, and sweetened. Pare, quarter, and take out the cores of the apples, when of a large size. If they are not ripe, stew them with just water enough to prevent their burning. When soft, sweeten and season them to the taste. When apples are ripe, they make better pies not to be stewed before baking. Fill your pie plates, cover them with a thick crust, and bake them from half to three-quarters of an hour. When baked sufficiently, cut the upper crust through the centre, remove it carefully with a broad knife, put a piece of butter, of the size of a walnut, into a pie, sweeten it to your taste, and if the apples are not tart enough, squeeze in the juice of part of a lemon—flavor the pie with either nutmeg, rosewater, or grated lemon peel. Apples cut into quarters, without paring, and stewed soft in new cider and molasses, make good plain pies. The apples should be strained after stewing, and seasoned with cinnamon or nutmeg. If made quite sweet, it will keep good several months. Dried apples should have boiling water turned on to cover them, and stewed till very soft. If they are not tart enough, turn in sour cider, when they are partly stewed. A little orange peel stewed with the apples, gives them a fine flavor. Season them, when soft, with sugar and nutmeg, and strain them if you like.

240. *Mince Pie.*

The best kind of meat for mince pies is neat's tongue and feet—the shank of beef makes very good pies. Boil the meat till perfectly tender—then take it up, clear it from the bones and gristle, chop it fine enough to strain through a sieve, mix it with an equal weight of tart apples, chopped very fine. If the meat is not fat, put in a little suet, or melted butter. Moisten the whole with cider—sweeten it to the taste with sugar, and very little molasses—add mace, cinnamon, cloves, and salt, to the taste. If you wish to make your pies rich, put in wine or brandy to the taste, and raisins, citron, and Zante currants. The grated rind and juice of lemons improve the pie. Make the pies on shallow plates, with apertures in the upper crust, and bake them from half to three-quarters of an hour, according to the heat of the oven. Meat prepared for pies in the following manner, will keep good several months, if kept in a cool dry place: To a pound of finely chopped meat, a quarter of a pound of suet, put half an ounce of mace, one ounce of cinnamon, a quarter of an ounce of cloves, two tea-spoonsful of salt. Add if you like the following fruits: half a pound of seeded raisins, half a pound of Zante currants, a quarter of a pound of citron. Put in half a pint of French brandy or wine, three table-spoonsful of molasses, and sugar sufficient to make it quite sweet. Put the whole in a stone pot—cover it with a paper wet in brandy. When you wish to use any of it for pies, put to what meat you use an equal weight of apples, pared and chopped fine. If not seasoned high enough, add more spice and sugar. If the apples are not tart, put in lemon-juice or sour cider.

241. *Rice Pie.*

To a quart of boiling water, put a small tea-cup of rice. Boil it till very soft, then take it from the fire, and add a quart of cold milk. Put in a tea-spoonful of salt, a grated nutmeg, five eggs beaten to a froth—add sugar to the taste, and strain it through a sieve. Bake it in deep pie plates, with an under crust and rim of pastry—add if you like a few raisins.

242. *Peach Pie.*

Take mellow, juicy peaches—wash and put them in a deep pie plate, lined with pie crust. Sprinkle a thick layer of sugar on each layer of peaches, put in about a table-spoonful of water, and sprinkle a little flour over the top—cover it with a thick crust, and bake the pie from fifty to sixty minutes. Pies made in this manner are much better than with the stones taken out, as the prussic acid of the stone gives the pie a fine flavor. If the peaches are not mellow, they will require stewing before being made into a pie. Dried peaches should be stewed soft, and sweetened, before they are made into a pie—they do not require any spice.

243. *Tart Pie.*

Sour apples, cranberries, and peaches, all make nice tarts. Stew, and strain them when soft. Peach tarts require a little lemon-juice, without they are sour. Grate in lemon peel, add brown sugar to the taste. Put in each pie one beaten egg, to make it cut smooth. Bake the pies on shallow plates, with an under crust and rim of pastry—ornament the pie with very small strips of pastry. When the crust is done, remove the pies from the oven.

244. *Rhubarb Pies.*

Take the tender stalks of the rhubarb, strip off the skin, and cut the stalks into thin slices. Line deep plates with pie crust, then put in the rhubarb, with a thick layer of sugar to each layer of rhubarb—a little grated lemon peel improves the pie. Cover the pies with a thick crust—press it down tight round the edge of the plate, and prick the crust with a fork, so that the crust will not burst while baking, and let out the juices of the pie. Rhubarb pies should be baked about an hour, in a slow oven—it will not do to bake them quick. Some cooks stew the rhubarb before making it into pies, but it is not so good as when used without stewing.

245. *Tomato Pie.*

Take green tomatoes, turn boiling water on them, and let them remain in it a few minutes—then strip off the skin, cut the tomatoes in slices, and put them in deep pie plates. Sprinkle sugar over each layer, and a little ginger.

Grated lemon peel, and the juice of a lemon, improve the pie. Cover the pies with a thick crust, and bake them slowly for about an hour.

246. *Lemon Pie.*

For one pie, take a couple of good sized fresh lemons, squeeze out the juice, and mix it with half a pint of molasses, or sufficient sugar to make the juice sweet. Chop the peel fine, line a deep pie plate with your pastry, then sprinkle on a layer of your chopped lemon peel, turn in part of the mixed sugar or molasses, and juice, then cover the whole with pie crust, rolled very thin—put in another layer of peel, sweetened juice, and crust, and so on, till all the lemon is used. Cover the whole with a thick crust, and bake the pie about half an hour.

247. *Cherry and Blackberry Pie.*

Cherries and blackberries for pies should be ripe. Bake them in deep pie plates, sweeten them with sugar, and put in cloves or cinnamon to the taste. Bake them about half an hour.

248. *Grape Pie.*

Grapes make the best pies when very tender and green. If not very small, they should be stewed and strained, to get out the seeds, before they are made into pies—sweeten them to the taste when stewed. They do not require any spice. If made into a pie without stewing, put to each layer of grapes a thick layer of sugar, and a table-spoonful of water.

249. *Currant and Gooseberry Pie.*

Currants and gooseberries are the best for pies when of a full growth, just before they begin to turn red—they are tolerably good when ripe. Currants mixed with ripe raspberries or mulberries, make very nice pies. Green currants and gooseberries for pies are not apt to be sweet enough without the sugar is scalded in before they are baked, as the juice of the currants is apt to run out while they are baking, and leave the fruit dry. Stew them on a moderate fire, with a tea-cup of water to a couple of quarts of currants—as soon as they begin to break, add the sugar, and let it scald in a few minutes. When baked without stewing, put to each layer of fruit a thick layer of sugar. There should be as much as a quarter of a pound of sugar to a pint of currants, to make them sufficiently sweet. Green currant pies are good sweetened with molasses and sugar mixed.

250. *Prune Pie.*

Prunes that are too dry to eat without stewing, can be made into good pies. Turn enough boiling water on the prunes to cover them, set them on a few coals, and let them remain till swelled out plump. If there is not water sufficient to make a nice syrup for the pies, add more, and season them with cinnamon or cloves. The juice and grated peel of a lemon gives them a fine flavor. Add sugar to the taste, and bake them in deep pie plates.

251. *Pumpkin Pie.*

Halve the pumpkin, take out the seeds—rinse the pumpkin, and cut it into small strips—stew them, over a moderate fire, in just sufficient water to prevent their burning, to the bottom of the pot. When stewed soft, turn off the water, and let the pumpkin steam, over a slow fire, for fifteen or twenty minutes, taking care that it does not burn. Take it from the fire, and strain it, when cool, through a sieve. If you wish to have the pies very rich, put to a quart of the stewed pumpkin two quarts of milk, and twelve eggs. If you like them plain, put to a quart of the pumpkin one quart of milk, and three eggs. The thicker the pie is of the pumpkin, the less will be the number of eggs required for them. One egg, with a table-spoonful of flour, will answer for a quart of the pumpkin, if very little milk is used. Sweeten the pumpkin with sugar, and very little molasses—the sugar and eggs should be beaten together. Ginger, the grated rind of a lemon, or nutmeg, is good spice for the pies. Pumpkin pies require a very hot oven. The rim of the pies is apt to get burnt before the inside is baked sufficiently. On this account, it is a good plan to heat the pumpkin scalding hot when prepared for pies, before turning it into the pie plates. The pies should be baked as soon as the plates are filled, or the under crust to the pies will be clammy. The more the number of eggs in the pies, the less time will be required to bake them. If you have pumpkins that have begun to decay, or those that are frozen, they can be kept several months, in cold weather, by cutting the good part up, stewing it till soft, then stirring it, and adding sugar and molasses, to make it very sweet. Make it strong of ginger, then scald the seasoning in well. Keep it in a stone jar, in a cool place—whenever you wish to use any of it for pies, take out the quantity you wish, and put milk and eggs to it.

252. *Carrot Pie.*

Scrape the skin off from the carrots, boil them soft, and strain them through a sieve. To a pint of the strained pulp put three pints of milk, six beaten eggs, two table-spoonsful of melted butter, the juice of half a lemon, and the grated rind of a whole one. Sweeten it to your taste, and bake it in deep pie plates without an upper crust.

253. *Potato Pie.*

Boil Carolina or mealy Irish potatoes, till very soft—when peeled, mash and strain them. To a quarter of a pound of potatoes, put a quart of milk, three table-spoonsful of melted butter, four beaten eggs, a wine glass of wine—add sugar and nutmeg to the taste.

254. *Sweet Marlborough Pie.*

Procure sweet mellow apples, pare and grate them. To a pint of the grated pulp put a pint of milk, a couple of eggs, two table-spoonsful of melted butter, the grated peel of a lemon, and half a wine glass of brandy. Sweeten it to the taste with nice brown sugar. The eggs should be beaten to a froth, then the sugar stirred into them, and mixed with the rest of the ingredients. A little stewed pumpkin, mixed with the apples, improves the pie. Bake the pie in deep plates, without an upper crust.

255. *Marlborough Tarts.*

Take tart juicy apples—quarter them, and stew them till soft enough to rub through a sieve. To twelve table-spoonsful of the strained apple, put twelve of sugar, the same quantity of wine, six table-spoonsful of melted butter, four beaten eggs, the juice and grated rind of a lemon, half a nutmeg, and half a pint of milk. Turn this, when the ingredients are well mixed together, into deep pie plates that are lined with pastry, and a rim of puff paste round the edge. Bake the tarts about half an hour.

256. *Cocoanut Pie.*

Cut off the brown part of the cocoanut—grate the white part, and mix it with milk, and set it on the fire, and let it boil slowly eight or ten minutes. To a pound of the grated cocoanut allow a quart of milk, eight eggs, four table-spoonsful of sifted white sugar, a glass of wine, a small cracker, pounded fine, two table-spoonsful of melted butter, and half a nutmeg. The eggs and sugar should be beaten together to a froth, then the wine stirred in. Put them into the milk and cocoanut, which should be first allowed to get quite cool—add the cracker and nutmeg—turn the whole into deep pie plates, with a lining and rim of puff paste. Bake them as soon as turned into the plates.

257. *Small Puffs.*

To make a dozen puffs, take a pound and a quarter of flour, a pound of butter, and one egg. Put them together according to the directions for puff pastry, [No. 238](). Divide it when made into three equal portions—roll one of them out half an inch thick, cut it into cakes with a tumbler—roll out the rest of the pastry, cut it into strips with a jagging iron, and lay the strips round those that are cut with a tumbler, so as to form a rim. Lay the puffs on buttered flat tins—bake them in a quick oven till a light brown, then fill them with any small preserved fruit you may happen to have.

258. *A Plain Custard Pie.*

Boil a quart of milk with half a dozen peach leaves, or the rind of a lemon. When they have flavored the milk, strain it, and set it where it will boil. Mix a table-spoonful of flour, smoothly, with a couple of table-spoonsful of milk, and stir it into the boiling milk. Let it boil a minute, stirring it constantly—take it from the fire, and when cool, put in three beaten eggs—sweeten it to the taste, turn it into deep pie plates, and bake the pies directly in a quick oven.

259. *A Rich Baked Custard.*

Beat seven eggs with three table-spoonsful of rolled sugar. When beaten to a froth, mix them with a quart of milk—flavor it with nutmeg. Turn it into cups, or else into deep pie plates, that have a lining and rim of pastry—bake them directly, in a quick oven. To ascertain when the custards are sufficiently baked, stick a clean broom splinter into them—if none of the custard adheres to the splinter, it is sufficiently baked.

260. *Boiled Custards.*

Put your milk on the fire, and let it boil up—then remove it from the fire, and let it cool. Beat for each quart of the milk, if liked rich, the yelks and half the whites of six eggs, with three table-spoonsful of rolled sugar—stir them into the milk when it is cool. If you wish to have your custards very plain, four eggs to a quart of the milk is sufficient. Season the custard with nutmeg or rosewater, and set it on a few coals, and stir it constantly until it thickens, and becomes scalding hot. Take it from the fire before it gets to boiling, and stir it a few minutes, then turn it into the cups. Beat the reserved whites of the eggs to a froth, and turn them on the top of the custards just before they are to be eaten.

261. *Mottled Custards.*

Stir into a quart of milk, while boiling, the beaten yelks of six eggs. Beat the whites of the eggs with three table-spoonsful of powdered white sugar, if the custards are liked very sweet—if not, a less quantity will answer. Stir in the whites of the eggs a minute after the yelks have set, so as to be thick. Season the custard with essence of lemon or rosewater—stir it till it becomes thick and lumpy, then turn it into cups.

262. *Cream Custards.*

Sweeten a pint of cream with powdered white sugar—set it on a few coals. When hot, stir in white wine until it curdles—add rosewater or essence of lemon to the taste, and turn it into cups. Another way of making them, which is very nice, is to mix a pint of cream with one of milk, five beaten eggs, a table-spoonful of flour, and three of sugar. Add nutmeg to the taste, and bake the custards in cups or pie plates, in a quick oven.

263. *Almond Custards.*

Blanch and pound fine, with a table-spoonful of rosewater, four ounces of almonds. Boil them four or five minutes in a quart of milk, with sufficient white sugar to sweeten the milk. Take it from the fire, and when lukewarm, stir in the beaten yelks of eight, and the whites of four eggs. Set the whole on the fire, and stir it constantly until it thickens—then take it up, stir it till partly cooled, and turn it into cups. If you wish to have the custards cool quick, set the cups into a pan of cold water—as fast as it gets warm, change it. Just before the custards are to be eaten, beat the reserved whites of the eggs to a froth, and cover the top of the custards with them.

264. *Apple Custards.*

Take half a dozen tart mellow apples—pare and quarter them, and take out the cores. Put them in a pan, with half a tea-cup of water—set them on a few coals. When they begin to grow soft, turn them into a pudding dish, sprinkle sugar on them. Beat eight eggs with rolled brown sugar—mix them with three pints of milk, grate in half a nutmeg, and turn the whole over the apples. Bake the custard between twenty and thirty minutes.

265. *Directions for making Puddings.*

A bag that is used for boiling puddings, should be made of thick cotton cloth. Before the pudding is turned in, the bag should be dipped into water, wrung out, and the inside of it floured. When the pudding is turned in, tie the bag tight, leaving plenty of room for the pudding to swell out in. Indian and flour puddings require a great deal of room. Put them in a pot of boiling water, with an old plate at the bottom of the pot, to keep the pudding bag from sticking to it. When the pudding has been in a few minutes, turn the bag over, or the pudding will settle, and be heavy. There should be water enough in the pot to cover the pudding, and it should not be allowed to stop boiling a minute—if so, the pudding will not be nice. A tea-kettle of boiling water should be kept on the fire, to turn in as the water boils away. When the pudding is done, dip the bag into cold water for a minute—the pudding will then come out easily. When puddings are baked, the fruit should not be put in till the pudding has begun to thicken, otherwise they will sink to the bottom of the pudding.

266. *Hasty Pudding.*

Wet sifted Indian meal with cold water, to make a thick batter. Stir it into a pot of boiling water gradually. Boil it an hour, then stir in sifted Indian meal, by the handful, till it becomes quite thick, and so that the pudding stick may be made to stand up in it. It should be stirred in very gradually, so that the pudding may not be lumpy. Add salt to the taste. Let it boil slowly, and stir it frequently, to keep it from burning on the inside of the pot. If you do not wish to fry the pudding, it will boil sufficiently in the course of an hour and a half. If it is to be fried, it will be necessary to boil it an hour longer; and a little flour stirred in, just before it is taken up, will make it fry better. It must get perfectly cold before it is fried. When you wish to fry it, cut it in slices half an inch thick, flour them, and fry them brown in a little lard.

267. *Corn Puddings.*

Grate sweet green corn—to three tea-cups of it, when grated, put two quarts of milk, eight eggs, a couple of tea-spoonsful of salt, half a tea-cup of melted butter, and a grated nutmeg. Bake the pudding an hour—serve it up with sauce.

268. *Cracker Pudding.*

Mix ten ounces of finely pounded crackers with a wine glass of wine, a little salt, and half a nutmeg, three or four table-spoonsful of sugar, two of melted butter. Beat eight eggs to a froth—mix them with three pints of milk, and turn them on to the rest of the ingredients. Let it remain till the crackers begin to soften, then bake it.

269. *Boiled Indian Pudding.*

Stir enough sifted Indian meal into a quart of boiling milk or water, to make a very stiff batter—then stir in a couple of table-spoonsful of flour, three of sugar or molasses, half a spoonful of ginger, or a couple of tea-spoonsful of cinnamon, and a couple of tea-spoonsful of salt. Two or three eggs improve the pudding, but are not essential—some people like a little chopped suet in them. The pudding will boil, so as to be very good, in the course of three hours, but it is better for being boiled five or six hours. Some cooks boil them eight or nine hours—when boiled so long, it is necessary to boil them several hours the day before they are to be eaten.

270. *Baked Indian Pudding.*

Boil a quart of milk, and turn it on to a pint of sifted Indian meal. Stir it in well, so as to scald the meal—then mix three table-spoonsful of wheat flour with a pint of milk. The milk should be stirred gradually into the flour, so as to have it mix free from lumps. Turn it on to the Indian meal—mix the whole well together. When the whole is just lukewarm, beat three eggs with three table-spoonsful of sugar—stir them into the pudding, together with two tea-spoonsful of salt, two of cinnamon, or a grated nutmeg, and a couple of table-spoonsful of melted butter, or suet chopped fine. Add, if you wish to have the pudding very rich, half a pound of raisins—they should not be put in till the pudding has baked five or six minutes. If raisins are put in, an additional half pint of milk will be required, as they absorb a great deal of milk. A very good Indian pudding may be made without eggs, if half a pint more of meal is used, and no flour. It takes three hours to bake an Indian pudding without eggs—if it has eggs in, it will bake in much less time.

271. *Minute Pudding.*

Put a pint and a half of milk on the fire. Mix five large table-spoonsful of either wheat or rye flour, smoothly, with half a pint of milk, a tea-spoonful of salt, and half of a grated nutmeg. When the milk boils, stir in the mixed flour and milk. Let the whole boil for one minute, stirring it constantly—take it from the fire, let it get lukewarm, then add three beaten eggs. Set it back on the fire, and stir it constantly until it thickens. Take it from the fire as soon as it boils.

272. *Boiled Bread Pudding.*

Take about three-quarters of a pound of bread, cut it into small pieces, and soak them soft in cold water—then drain off the water, mash the bread fine, and mix with it two table-spoonsful of flour, three eggs, a tea-spoonful of salt, a table-spoonful of melted butter, and cold milk sufficient to make it a thick batter. Mix the whole well together, then turn it into a floured pudding bag—tie it up, so as to leave room for the pudding to swell—boil it an hour and a half, without any intermission. Serve up the pudding with rich sauce.

273. *A Plain Baked Bread Pudding.*

Pound rusked bread fine—to five heaping table-spoonsful of it, put a quart of milk, three beaten eggs, three table-spoonsful of rolled sugar, a tea-spoonful of salt, half a nutmeg, and three table-spoonsful of melted butter. Bake it about an hour—it does not need any sauce.

274. *Rich Bread Pudding.*

Cut a pound loaf of bakers' bread into thin slices—spread butter on them as for eating—lay them in a pudding dish—sprinkle between each layer of bread seeded raisins, and citron, cut in small strips. Beat eight eggs with four table-spoonsful of rolled sugar—mix them with three pints of milk, half of a grated nutmeg. Turn the whole on to the bread, and let it remain until the bread has absorbed full half of the milk—then bake it about three-quarters of an hour.

275. *Flour Pudding.*

Into a pint and a half of sifted flour stir gradually, so that it may not be lumpy, a quart of milk. Beat seven eggs, and put in, together with a couple of table-spoonsful of melted butter, and a couple of tea-spoonsful of salt. Grate in half of a nutmeg—add, if you want the pudding very rich, half a pound of raisins. They should not be put into a baked pudding till it has been cooking long enough to thicken, so that the raisins will not sink to the bottom of it. A pudding made in this manner is good either baked or boiled. It takes two hours to boil, and an hour and a quarter to bake it. When boiled, the bag should not be more than two-thirds full, as flour puddings swell very much. It should be put into boiling water, and kept boiling constantly. If the water boils away, so as to leave any part of the bag uncovered, more boiling water should be added. When the pudding has boiled eight or nine minutes, the bag should be turned over, otherwise the pudding will be heavy. Flour puddings should be eaten as soon as cooked, as they fall directly. Serve them up with rich sauce.

276. *Boiled Rice Pudding.*

Put two tea-cups of rice into a quart of boiling water—add a couple of tea-spoonsful of salt, and let the rice boil till soft. Then take it from the fire, stir in a quart of cold milk, and half a pound of raisins; or omit the raisins, and substitute any other fruit that you may like. Beat a couple of eggs, and put in, together with half of a grated nutmeg. Set the whole on the fire, and let it boil till the fruit is soft. Serve it up with butter and sugar.

277. *A Baked Rice Pudding, without eggs.*

Pick over and wash two small tea-cups of rice, and put it into two quarts of milk. Melt a small tea-cup of butter, and put in, together with two of sugar, a grated nutmeg, and a couple of tea-spoonsful of salt, and bake the pudding about two hours. This pudding does not need any sauce, and is good either hot or cold. If you wish to have the pudding very rich, add, when it has been baking five or six minutes, half a pound of raisins.

278. *Rice Pudding, with eggs.*

Boil a quarter of a pound of unground rice in a quart of milk till soft, then stir in a quarter of a pound of butter—take it from the fire, put in a pint of cold milk, a couple of tea-spoonsful of salt, and a grated nutmeg. When it is lukewarm, beat four eggs with a quarter of a pound of sugar, and stir it into the pudding—add half a pound of raisins, and turn the whole into a buttered pudding dish, and bake it three-quarters of an hour.

279. *Ground Rice Pudding.*

Mix a pint and a half of ground rice, smooth, with a quart of milk—stir in a glass of wine, a quarter of a pound of melted butter, a tea-spoonful of salt, and spice to the taste. Beat eight eggs, and stir them in—turn the whole into a buttered pudding dish, and when it has baked a few minutes, add half a pound of raisins, or Zante currants.

280. *Rice Snow Balls.*

Pare small, tart apples, and take out the cores with a small knife—fill the cavity with a stick of cinnamon or mace. Put each one in a small floured bag, and fill the bags about half full of unground rice. Tie up the bags so as to leave a great deal of room for the rice to swell. Put them in a pot of water, with a table-spoonful of salt to a couple of quarts of water. The bags of rice should be boiled in a large proportion of water, as the rice absorbs it very much. Boil them about an hour and twenty minutes, then turn them out of the bags carefully into a dessert dish, and garnish them with marmalade cut in slices. Serve them up with butter and sugar.

281. *Cream Pudding.*

Beat six eggs to a froth—then mix with them three table-spoonsful of powdered white sugar, the grated rind of a lemon. Mix a pint of milk with a pint of flour, two tea-spoonsful of salt—then add the eggs and sugar. Just before it is baked, stir in a pint of thick cream. Bake it either in buttered cups or a pudding dish.

282. *Custard Pudding.*

Stir a quart of milk very gradually into half a pint of flour—mix it free from lumps, and put to it seven eggs, beaten with three table-spoonsful of sugar, a tea-spoonful of salt, and half of a grated nutmeg. Bake it three-quarters of an hour.

283. *Rennet Pudding.*

Put cleaned calf's rennet into white wine, in the proportion of a piece three inches square to a pint of wine. It will be fit for use in the course of seven or eight hours. Whenever you wish to make a pudding, put three table-spoonsful of the wine to a quart of sweet milk, and four table-spoonsful of powdered white sugar—flavor it with rosewater or essence of lemon. Stir it twenty minutes, then dish it out, and grate nutmeg over it. It should be eaten in the course of an hour after it is made, as it soon curdles.

284. *Fruit Pudding.*

Make good common pie crust—roll it out half an inch thick, and strew over it any one of the following kinds of fruit: Cherries, currants, gooseberries, strawberries, raspberries, blackberries, or cranberries. A thick layer of marmalade spread on, is also very nice. Sprinkle over the fruit a little cinnamon or cloves, and sugar. If the pudding is made of gooseberries, currants, or cranberries, a great deal of sugar will be necessary. Roll the crust up carefully, join the ends so that the fruit will not drop out, and lay the pudding in a thick white towel, that has been previously dipped into water, and floured. Baste up the towel, and lay it carefully in a pot of boiling water, with a plate at the bottom of it. Boil it an hour, and serve it up with rich liquid sauce. For a baked fruit pudding, make a batter of wheat flour, or Indian meal, with milk and eggs. Mix the ingredients in the proportion of a pint of flour and six eggs to a quart of milk. Put to each quart of milk a pint of fruit, and sugar to the taste.

285. *A Quaking Pudding.*

Slice up three-quarters of a pound of bakers' bread. Beat eight eggs to a froth, stir in several large spoonsful of sugar, and mix it with a quart of milk, a grated nutmeg. Turn it on to the sliced bread—let the whole remain till the bread has soaked up most of the milk, then stir in a couple of table-spoonsful of flour, a tea-spoonful of salt, and turn it into a pudding bag, and boil it an hour. Serve it up with rich sauce.

286. *Lemon Pudding.*

Grate the rind of two fresh lemons, being careful not to grate any off the white part. Squeeze the juice out of the lemons, and strain it, to separate it from the seeds. Mix it with six large spoonsful of fine white sugar. Take a quart of milk, and mix it with the rind of the lemons, a couple of table-spoonsful of pounded crackers, and a table-spoonful of melted butter. Beat six eggs to a froth, and stir them into the milk. Stir in the lemon-juice and sugar last, and then turn the whole into a pudding dish that has a lining and rim of puff paste. Bake it from twenty-five to thirty minutes. It should not be eaten till it is cold.

287. *Almond Pudding.*

Turn boiling water on three-quarters of a pound of sweet almonds. Let them remain in it till the skins will slip off easily—rub the skins off with a dry cloth. When they are perfectly dry, pound them fine, with a table-spoonful of rosewater. Beat six eggs to a froth, then mix them with four table-spoonsful of powdered sugar—put them into a quart of milk, with three table-spoonsful of pounded crackers, a quarter of a pound of melted butter, four ounces of citron, and the pounded almonds. Line a pudding dish with pastry, put round it a rim of puff paste, turn in the pudding, and bake it about half an hour. The pudding should be eaten cold.

288. *Tapioca Pudding.*

To a quart of warm milk put eight table-spoonsful of tapioca. Let it soak till it softens, then stir it up, and put to it a couple of table-spoonsful of melted butter, four beaten eggs, and cinnamon or mace to the taste. Mix four table-spoonsful of white powdered sugar with a wine glass of wine, and stir it into the rest of the ingredients. Turn the whole into a pudding dish that has a lining of pastry, and bake it immediately.

289. *Sago Pudding.*

Rinse half a pound of sago in hot water, till it is thoroughly cleansed—then drain off the water, and boil the sago in a quart of milk, with a stick of cinnamon or mace. Stir it constantly, or it will burn. When soft, take it from the fire, take out the stick of cinnamon, and put in a quarter of a pound of butter. Mix a wine glass of wine with four large spoonsful of fine white sugar, and stir it into the sago—add, when cold, five beaten eggs, and bake the pudding in a deep dish, with a lining and rim of pastry. Strew over the pudding a quarter of a pound of Zante currants, and bake it directly, in a quick oven. It is the best when cold.

290. *Orange Pudding.*

Stir to a cream six ounces of white powdered sugar, with four of butter—then add a wine glass of wine, the juice and chopped peel of a couple of large fresh oranges. Beat eight eggs to a froth, the whites and yelks separately—mix them with a quart of milk, a couple of ounces citron, cut in small strips, and a couple of ounces of pounded crackers. Mix all the ingredients well together—line a pudding dish with pastry, put a rim of puff paste round the edge of the dish, and then turn in the pudding, and bake it in a quick oven about half an hour.

291. *Bird's Nest, or Transparent Pudding.*

Pare and halve tart mellow apples, scoop out the cores. Put a little flour and water in the hollow of each apple, so as to form a thick paste—then stick three or four Zante currants in each one. Butter and line a pudding dish with pastry, put on a rim of puff paste, and lay in the apples, with the hollow side up. Have just enough apples to cover the bottom of the dish, and stick citron, cut in very long narrow strips, round the apples. Stir to a cream half a pound each of butter and fine white sugar—beat the yelks and whites separately, of eight eggs, to a froth, and mix them with the butter and sugar. Flavor it with nutmeg, and set it on a few coals—stir it constantly till quite hot—take it from the fire, stir it till nearly cold, then turn it over the apples, and bake it directly.

292. *English Plum Pudding.*

Soak three-quarters of a pound of crackers in two quarts of milk—they should be broken in small pieces. When they have soaked soft, put in a quarter of a pound of melted butter, the same weight of rolled sugar, half a pint of wheat flour, a wine glass of wine, and a grated nutmeg. Beat ten eggs to a froth, and stir them into the milk. Add half a pound of seeded raisins, the same weight of Zante currants, and a quarter of a pound of citron, cut in small strips. Bake or boil it a couple of hours.

293. *Plain Fritters.*

Stir a quart of milk gradually into a quart of flour—put in a tea-spoonful of salt, and seven beaten eggs. Drop them by the large spoonful into hot lard, and fry them till a very light brown color. They are the lightest fried in a great deal of fat, but less greasy if fried in just fat enough to keep them from sticking to the frying pan. Serve them up with liquid pudding sauce.

294. *Apple Fritters.*

Take four or five tart, mellow apples, pare and cut them in slices, and soak them in sweetened lemon-juice. Make a batter of a quart of milk, a quart of flour, eight eggs—grate in the rind of two lemons, and the juice and apples. Drop the batter by the spoonful into hot lard, taking care to have a slice of apple in each fritter.

295. *Cream Fritters.*

Mix a pint and a half of wheat flour with a pint of milk—beat six eggs to a froth, and stir them into the flour—grate in half a nutmeg, then add a pint of cream, a couple of tea-spoonsful of salt. Stir the whole just long enough to have the cream get well mixed in, then fry the mixture in small cakes.

296. *Oxford Dumplings.*

Take eight ounces of biscuit that is pounded fine, and soak it in just sufficient milk to cover it. When soft, stir in three beaten eggs, a table-spoonful of flour, and a quarter of a pound of Zante currants. Grate in half a nutmeg, and do up the mixture into balls of the size of an egg—fry them till a light brown.

297. *Apple Dumplings.*

Pare tart, mellow apples—take out the cores with a small knife, and fill the holes with sugar. Make good pie crust—roll it out about two-thirds of an inch thick, cut it into pieces just large enough to enclose one apple. Lay the apples on them, and close the crust tight over them—tie them up in small pieces of thick cloth, that has been well floured—put the dumplings in a pot of boiling water, and boil them an hour without any intermission—if allowed to stop boiling, they will be heavy. Serve them up with pudding sauce, or butter and sugar.

298. *Lemon Syrup.*

Pare thin the rind of fresh lemons, squeeze out the juice, and to a pint of it, when strained, put a pound and three-quarters of sugar, and the rind of the lemons. Dissolve the sugar by a gentle heat, skim it clear, then let it simmer gently eight or ten minutes—strain it through a flannel bag. When cool, bottle, cork, and seal it tight, and keep it in a cool place.

299. *Orange Syrup.*

Squeeze out the juice of fresh oranges, and strain it. To a pint of the juice, put a pound and a half of sugar—set it on a moderate fire—when the sugar has dissolved, put in the peel of the oranges, and set the syrup where it will boil slowly for six or eight minutes—then strain it, till clear, through a flannel bag. The bag should not be squeezed while the syrup is passing through it, or it will not be clear. Bottle, cork, and seal it tight. This syrup is very nice to flavor puddings and pies.

300. *Blackberry Syrup.*

Procure nice, high vine blackberries, that are perfectly ripe—the low vine blackberries will not answer for syrup, as they do not possess the medicinal properties of the high vine blackberries. Set them on a moderate fire, and let them simmer till they break to pieces, then strain them through a flannel cloth—to each pint of juice put a pound of white sugar, half an ounce of cinnamon, powdered fine, a quarter of an ounce of finely powdered mace, and a couple of tea-spoonsful of powdered cloves. Boil the whole together fifteen minutes—strain it, and when cool, add to each pint of syrup a wine glass of French brandy. Bottle, cork, and seal it—keep it in a cool place. This, mixed with cold water, in the proportion of a wine glass of syrup to two-thirds of a tumbler of water, is an excellent remedy for the dysentery, and similar complaints. It is also a very pleasant summer beverage.

301. *Elderberry Syrup.*

Wash and strain the berries, which should be perfectly ripe. To a pint of juice, put a pint of molasses. Boil it twenty minutes, stirring it constantly, then take it from the fire—when cold, add to each quart four tablespoonsful of French brandy—bottle and cork it tight. This is an excellent remedy for a tight cough.

302. *Molasses Syrup, for preserving.*

Mix eight pounds of light sugar-house or New-Orleans molasses, eight pounds of water, one pound of powdered charcoal. Boil the whole together twenty minutes, then strain it through a flannel bag. When lukewarm, put in the beaten whites of a couple of eggs, and put it on the fire. As soon as it boils, take it from the fire, and skim it till clear—then put it on the fire, and let it boil till it becomes a thick syrup—strain it for use. This syrup does very well to preserve fruit in for common use.

303. *To clarify Syrup for Sweetmeats.*

Put your sugar into the preserving kettle, turn in the quantity of cold water that you think will be sufficient to cover the fruit that is to be preserved in it. Beat the whites of eggs to a froth, allowing one white of an egg to three pounds of sugar—mix the whites of the eggs with the sugar and water, set it on a slow fire, and let the sugar dissolve, then stir the whole up well together, and set it where it will boil. As soon as it boils up well, take it from the fire, let it remain for a minute, then take off the scum—set it back on the fire, and let it boil a minute, then take it off, and skim it again. This operation repeat till the syrup is clear—put in the fruit when the syrup is cold. The fruit should not be crowded while preserving, and if there is not syrup enough to cover the fruit, take it out of the syrup, and put in more water, and boil it with the syrup before putting back the fruit.

304. *Directions for making Sweetmeats.*

A pound of sugar to a pound of fruit, is sufficient to preserve most kinds of fruit. Some kinds of fruit require more, and some will do with less, than an equal weight of sugar. White sugar makes the most delicate sweetmeats

—nice brown sugar answers very well for most kinds of fruit. The West India sugar-house syrup is better than sugar to preserve fruit, on account of its never fermenting. When brown sugar is used, clarify it, as in direction for clarifying syrup, No. 303, then put in the fruit. Nice white sugar does not need clarifying. All kinds of fire-proof ware will do to preserve in, excepting iron ware. The fruit should not be crowded while preserving, and should boil gently. The fruit should be turned out of the preserving kettles as soon as done, and set away in a cool place, otherwise they will not be nice. Keep the sweetmeats in stone or china jars, that have never been used for other purposes. Glass jars are the best for delicate sweetmeats, such as strawberries or cherries. Preserves should be covered tight, and kept in a cool place. A paper wet in brandy, and laid over the sweetmeats, has a tendency to keep them from fermenting. They should be looked to frequently, to see that they do not ferment. Whenever they do, the syrup should be turned from them, scalded, and turned back on them while hot.

305. *To Preserve Quinces.*

Quinces, if very ripe, are best preserved in the following manner: Pare and cut them in slices, an inch thick—take out the cores carefully, so as to have the slices in the form of a ring. Allow a pound of nice white sugar for each pound of the fruit—dissolve it in cold water, having a quart of the latter to a pound of sugar, then put in the sliced quinces, and let them soak in it ten or twelve hours. Put them in a preserving kettle, and put it on a moderate fire—cover them over, and let the quinces boil gently—there should be more than enough syrup to cover the quinces. When a broom splinter will go through them easily, take them from the fire, and turn them out. In the course of a week, turn the syrup from them, and boil it down, so that there will be just enough to cover the fruit. Quinces preserved in this manner retain their natural flavor better than when preserved in any other manner, but they must be very ripe to preserve in this way, otherwise they will not be tender. When not very ripe, pare and cut them either in rings or quarters, take out the cores, and boil the quinces in fair water, till they begin to grow tender—take them up, and strain the water in which they are boiled—put in either brown or white sugar—add a little cold water. When lukewarm, put in the whites of eggs, and clarify it—let it cool, then put in the quinces, and boil them slowly for half an hour. Keep them covered over while boiling, if you wish to have them of a light color. Turn them out into pots as soon as preserved, and set them away in a cool place. Look at them in the course of a week, to see if they have fermented—if so, turn the syrup from them, boil it, and turn it back while hot. The parings and cores of the quinces can be used for marmalade, with a few whole ones. Some people preserve the quinces with the cores in, but the syrup will not look clear. The following is a cheap method of preserving quinces, and answers very well for common use: Pare, halve, and take out the cores of the quinces, and boil the parings in new cider till soft. Strain the cider, and for five pounds of quinces put in a pound of brown sugar, a quart of molasses, the beaten white of an egg—clarify it, then put in the quinces. There should be rather more than enough cider to cover the quinces, as it wastes a good deal while the quinces are boiling. The peel of an orange, cut in small pieces, and boiled with them, gives the quinces a fine flavor.

306. *Quince Marmalade.*

Wash and quarter the quinces, without paring them—put them on the fire, with just water enough to stew them in. When soft, rub them through a sieve, and put to each pound of the strained quinces a pound of brown sugar. Set it on a few coals, and let it stew slowly, stirring it constantly. When it has stewed an hour, take a little of it out, let it get cold—if it then cuts smooth, it is sufficiently stewed.

307. *Pears.*

Make a syrup, allowing three-quarters of a pound of sugar to each pound of the pears. If brown sugar is used for the syrup, clarify it, then put in the pears, and boil them till soft. A few slips of ginger, or powdered ginger, tied up in bags, and boiled with the pears, gives them a fine flavor. Choke and vergouleuse are the best pears for preserving.

308. *Pear Marmalade.*

Boil the pears with the skins on. When soft, rub them through a sieve, and put to each pound of pulp three-quarters of a pound of brown sugar.

Stew it over a slow fire till it becomes a thick jelly. It should be stirred constantly.

309. *Peaches.*

Take juicy peaches—pare them, allow for each pound of them, a pound of nice white sugar. Put just cold water enough to the sugar to saturate it. When dissolved, stir it up well, and put in the peaches, without crowding them, and boil them slowly about twenty minutes. A few peach meats, blanched and preserved with the peaches, are nice, and are quite ornamental to the peaches. These, as well as all other kinds of sweetmeats, should be turned out of the preserving kettle as soon as taken from the fire, and set away in a cool place. If allowed to remain near the fire, the syrup will not look clear. Cover them up tight—let them remain three or four days, then turn the syrup from them, scald it, and turn it back, while hot, on to the peaches.

310. *Peach Jam.*

Inferior peaches, and those that are not fully ripe, are best preserved in the following manner: Pare and halve them, and take out the stones—lay the peaches in a deep dish, and to each layer of peaches put a layer of brown sugar. Three-quarters of a pound of sugar to a pound of the peaches, is sufficient. Let the peaches remain until the next day—then put them on a moderate fire, without any water, and let them stew slowly about twenty minutes. Peaches preserved in this way, are very nice for puffs.

311. *To Preserve Peaches in Brandy.*

Procure peaches that are mellow, but not dead ripe—draw a pin round the seam of the peaches, so as to pierce the skin—cover them with French brandy, and let them remain a week—then make a syrup, allowing three-quarters of a pound of brown sugar to a pound of the peaches. Clarify the syrup, then boil the peaches in it. When tender, take them out of the syrup, let it remain till cool, then mix it with the brandy, and turn the whole on to the peaches.

312. *To Preserve Raspberries.*

Strain equal quantities of ripe currants and raspberries, to make a syrup to preserve the raspberries in. Dissolve white sugar in the syrup, by a gentle heat, using a pound of sugar to each pound of syrup and raspberries. When the sugar has dissolved, set the syrup where it will boil about ten minutes, then put in the raspberries, and let them boil five minutes. In the course of four or five days, turn the syrup from the raspberries—boil it away, so that there will be just enough of it to cover the berries—turn it on them while hot. Keep them in wide-mouthed bottles, corked and sealed up tight. Preserved raspberries are very nice to flavor ice creams and blanc mange.

313. *Cherries.*

Procure cherries that are not quite dead ripe—allow for each pound of cherries a pound of white sugar. Make a rich syrup of the sugar—when it boils, put in the cherries, with the stems on—let them boil till transparent. Keep them in glass jars, or wide-mouthed bottles—cork and seal them tight. If you wish to preserve them without the stones, take those that are very ripe, take out the stones carefully, save the juice. Make a syrup of the juice, white sugar, and very little water, then put in the cherries, and boil them to a thick consistency.

314. *Currants.*

Take the currants when ripe and in their prime—let them remain on the stalks, picking off the bad ones. Make a syrup of sugar, and very little water, allowing a pound of sugar to each pound of currants. Clarify it, then put in the currants, and let them boil a few minutes. In the course of a few days turn the syrup from them, scald it, and turn it back, while hot, on to the currants. Preserved currants, mixed with water, is an excellent drink in fevers. Dried currants are also good for the same purpose, if made into a tea.

315. *To Preserve Prunes.*

Pour boiling water on the prunes, and set them where they will keep hot, with a lemon, cut in small pieces. When swelled out to nearly the original size, put to each pound of the prunes half a pound of brown sugar, a stick of cinnamon, or a tea-spoonful of powdered cloves, and if there is not sufficient water remaining to cover the prunes, add more, and stew them in the syrup a quarter of an hour. Add, when taken from the fire, a wine glass of wine to every three pounds of the prunes.

316. *Cranberries.*

For each peck of cranberries allow two pounds and a half of brown sugar, and half a pint of molasses. Make a syrup of the molasses, sugar, and a little water. When it boils, put in the cranberries, and let them boil till transparent. To make cranberry marmalade, boil the cranberries in just water enough to prevent their burning. Strain them when soft, and add to each pound a pound and a half of brown sugar. Stew it over a slow fire, stirring it constantly, till it becomes very thick jelly.

317. *Crab Apples.*

Make a syrup, allowing the same weight of sugar as apples. Let it get cool, then put in the apples, a few at once, so that they will not crowd, and break to pieces. Boil them till they begin to break, then take them out of the preserving kettle carefully. Boil the syrup in the course of three or four days, and turn it while hot on to the apples. This continue to do at intervals of two or three days, till the apples appear to be thoroughly preserved. If you wish to make a marmalade of the apples, boil them in just water enough to keep them from burning—strain them when soft, and put to them an equal weight of brown sugar—stew them over a slow fire, stirring them constantly. When of a thick consistency, take a little of it out, and set it where it will get cold. If it then cuts smooth and clear, take the whole from the fire, and turn it into deep dishes.

318. *Barberries.*

Take them when fully ripe, let them remain on the stems. Make a rich syrup, allowing the same weight of sugar as barberries. When clarified, set it where it will get lukewarm, then put in the barberries. Boil them till the syrup appears to have entered them. Barberries preserved with molasses, and a little orange peel and sugar, are very good for common use. Allow for each pound of barberries a quarter of a pound of sugar, half a pint of molasses, and the rind of half an orange. Make them into a syrup with a little water—boil it a quarter of an hour before putting in the barberries. Preserved barberries, mixed with cold water, make a very refreshing drink in fevers.

319. *Tomatoes.*

Take them when quite small and green—put them in cold clarified syrup, with an orange, cut in slices, to every two pounds of the tomatoes. Simmer them gently, on a slow fire, two or three hours. There should be equal weights of sugar and tomatoes, and more than sufficient water to cover the tomatoes, used for the syrup. Another method of preserving them, which is very nice, is to allow a couple of fresh lemons to three pounds of the tomatoes—pare thin the rind of the lemons, so as to get none of the white part, squeeze out the juice, mix them with cold water sufficient to cover the tomatoes, and put in a few peach leaves, and powdered ginger, tied up in bags. Boil the whole together gently, for three-quarters of an hour—then take up the tomatoes, strain the liquor, and put to it a pound and a half of white sugar, for each pound of tomatoes. Put in the tomatoes, and boil them gently, till the syrup appears to have entered them. In the course of a week turn the syrup from them, heat it scalding hot, and turn it on to the tomatoes. Tomatoes preserved in this manner appear like West Indian sweetmeats.

320. *To Preserve Apples.*

Apples for preserving should be tart and mellow—pare them, and take out the cores with a small knife. Allow for each pound three-quarters of a pound of sugar, a tea-spoonful of powdered ginger, tied in a bag, and sufficient water to cover the apples. Make the syrup, then take it from the fire, and put in the apples, when it is just lukewarm. Boil them till transparent, take them up—when partly cooled, put in a little essence of lemon. Turn the syrup from them in the course of a week, boil it, and turn it back on the apples while hot.

321. *Cymbelines, or Mock Citron.*

Cut into small pieces, and scrape the rind of cymbelines—put them into strong salt and water—let them remain in it three days, then in fair water a day, changing the water several times—soak them in alum water an hour—tie up oyster shells in a cloth, and boil them with the cymbelines. When the cymbelines are tender, take them up, and put them back into the alum water. Make the syrup for them, allowing a pound and a half of sugar to one of the cymbelines. When clarified, let it get cold—then rinse the cymbelines, and boil them three-quarters of an hour. When partly cooled, put in a little essence of lemon to flavor them. These are good eaten like any other sweetmeats, or used instead of citron for cake.

322. *Watermelon Rinds.*

Take the rind of a nice ripe watermelon—cut it into small strips, and boil them, till they begin to grow tender, in water, with saleratus and peach leaves in it, in the proportion of a tea-spoonful of saleratus and a dozen peach leaves to a couple of quarts of water. Take the rinds out of the water, and soak them in alum water an hour. Make a syrup, allowing the same weight of sugar as rinds. When clarified and cooled, rinse the rinds, and put them in the syrup, together with powdered ginger, tied up in a small bag. Boil them till they are quite soft—when partly cooled, add a little essence of lemon. Turn the syrup from them in the course of two or three days, take out the bags of ginger, and boil the syrup till there is just sufficient of it to cover the rinds, and turn it on them while hot.

323. *Muskmelons.*

Procure muskmelons that are perfectly green, and of a quick growth, and as late in the season as possible. If preserved while the weather is very hot, they are apt to ferment. Scrape off the skin of the rind, being careful not to scrape any of the green part. Cut them through the middle, and take out the seeds—then cut them in rings, an inch in thickness. Soak them in salt and water a day, then in fair water three or four hours, changing the water several times. Soak them in alum water an hour—rinse and put them in fair water, with a handful of peach leaves to four or five pounds of the melon, and a table-spoonful of ginger, tied up in small pieces of cloth. The peach leaves turn the melon a fine green color. Boil the melons till they begin to grow tender, then put them in alum water, together with the ginger. Make a syrup of white sugar, and put in the melons and ginger, (which should be previously rinsed.) Boil them in the syrup as long as you can, without their breaking to pieces. In the course of a week turn the syrup from them, scald it, and turn it on to the melons. Add sufficient essence of lemon to flavor it, just before turning it on to the melons. Keep them covered tight, in a cool place, with a paper wet in brandy on them.

324. *Pine Apples.*

Take those that are ripe, and perfectly fresh—pare off the rind, and cut the apples in slices an inch thick. Powder the same weight of white sugar as you have pine apples—lay the pine apples in a deep dish, and sprinkle part of the powdered sugar between each layer of apples. Reserve about half of the sugar. Let the apples remain till the succeeding day—then turn the syrup from them, and mix it with the reserved sugar, and half a pint of water, for three or four pounds of pine apple. Boil the syrup, take it from the fire, and when cool, put in the apples, simmer them gently till tender, let them remain in a deep dish for several days—they should be covered up tight, and kept in a cool place. Whenever there is any appearance of fermentation, turn the syrup from them, scald it, and turn it back hot on to the pine apples. Keep them in glass or china jars, covered tight, and in a cool place.

325. *Pumpkin Chips.*

Take what quantity you choose of a good sweet pumpkin, (the butter pumpkin makes the nicest sweetmeats.) Halve the pumpkin, take out the seeds, and cut it into chips of the size of a dollar. For each pound of the pumpkin to be preserved, allow a pound of fine white sugar, and a gill of lemon-juice. Put the chips in a deep dish, and sprinkle on each layer a layer of the sugar. Turn the lemon-juice over the whole. Let it remain a day—then boil the whole together, with half a pint of water to three pounds of the pumpkin, a table-spoonful of powdered ginger, tied up in bags, and the peel of the lemons, cut into small pieces. When the pumpkin becomes tender, turn the whole into a preserve pot. In the course of a week, turn the syrup from the pumpkin, boil it to a rich syrup, and turn it back hot.

326. *Gages.*

Allow equal weights of sugar and gages. Make a syrup of white sugar, and just water enough to cover the plums. Boil the plums slowly in the syrup ten minutes—turn them into a dish, and let them remain four or five days, then boil them again, till the syrup appears to have entered the plums. Put them in a china jar, and in the course of a week turn the syrup from them, scald it, and turn it over them hot.

327. *Strawberries.*

Procure Chili or field strawberries, and hull them. Take equal quantities of berries, and powdered white sugar—put a layer of each in a preserving pan, having a layer of strawberries at the bottom. Let them remain an hour, then put in a gill of cold water, to prevent their burning to the bottom of the pan. Set them on a very moderate fire—when the juice runs freely, increase the fire, until they boil briskly. Let them boil half an hour, then turn them into a dish—when lukewarm, put them in wide-mouthed bottles, or small glass jars, cork and seal them tight, and keep them in dry sand.

328. *Raspberry and Blackberry Jam.*

For each pound of berries, allow a pound of sugar. Put a layer of each alternately in a preserving dish. Let them remain half an hour—then boil them slowly, stirring them frequently, to keep them from burning. When they have boiled half an hour, take a little up in a cup, and set it in a dish of cold water—if it appears of the consistency of thick jelly, take the whole from the fire—if not, boil it till it becomes so.

329. *Strawberry, Raspberry, and Blackberry Jelly.*

Jellies of these fruits are all made in the following manner: Take the berries when ripe, and in their prime, mash them, and let them drain through a flannel bag, without squeezing it. To each pint of juice, put a pound of white sugar, and the beaten white of an egg to three pounds of the sugar. Set it on the fire—when it boils up well, take it from the fire, and skim it clear. Set it back on the fire—if any more scum rises, take it from the fire, and skim it off. Boil it till it becomes a jelly, which is ascertained by taking a little of it up into a tumbler of cold water. If it falls to the bottom in a solid mass, it is sufficiently boiled.

330. *Cranberry, Grape, and Currant Jelly.*

They are all made in the same manner. Take the fruit in its prime, wash and drain it till nearly dry, then put it in an earthen jar, or pot, and set the pot in a kettle of hot water. Set the kettle where the water will boil, taking care that none of it gets into the jar. When the fruit breaks, turn it into a flannel bag, and let it drain slowly through, into a deep dish, without squeezing. When the juice has all passed through the bag, put to each pint of it a pound and a half of white sugar. Put to each quart of the syrup the beaten white of an egg. Set the syrup where it will boil gently—as fast as any scum rises, take the syrup from the fire, and skim it clear. When the jelly has boiled fifteen or twenty minutes, try a little of it in a tumbler of cold water—if it sinks to the bottom of the tumbler in a solid lump, it is sufficiently boiled. Jellies are improved by being put in the sun for several days—care must be taken that the dew does not fall on them.

331. *Quince Jelly.*

Halve the quinces, and take out the cores. Boil the quinces till very soft, in clear water, mash them, and let them drain through a flannel bag, without squeezing them. Put to the quince liquor, when drained through the bag, white sugar, in the proportion of a pound to a pint of the liquor. Add the whites of eggs, and clarify it. When clear, boil it on a moderate fire, till it becomes a thick jelly. Fill glasses with the jelly, and cover them tight. The quince pulp that remains in the jelly-bag can be made into marmalade.

332. *Apple Jelly.*

Halve tart apples, and take out the cores. Boil them till very soft, in a large proportion of water—then let it pass through a jelly-bag, without squeezing them. Weigh the liquor, and to each pint of it put a pound of white sugar—then boil it slowly till it becomes a thick jelly, which is ascertained in the same manner as currant jelly. If you wish to have it of a red tinge, put in, when taken from the fire, a little cranberry or beet-juice. If you wish to have it a straw color, put in a little tincture of saffron. If green, use the expressed juice of spinach leaves. Let it pass through the jelly-bag again—when cool, turn it into glasses.

333. *Lemon Jelly.*

Put on a slow fire an ounce of white isinglass, pulled into small pieces, and rinsed, a pint of water, with the rind of six lemons. Stir it constantly till dissolved, then add a pint of lemon-juice, and sweeten it to the taste with nice white sugar. Boil the whole four or five minutes, then color it with tincture of saffron, and let it pass through a flannel bag, without squeezing it. Fill your jelly glasses with it when partly cooled.

334. *Calf's Feet Jelly.*

Take four feet, (that have been perfectly cleaned,) and boil them, in four quarts of water, till very soft, and the water is reduced to one quart. Take it from the fire, and let it remain till perfectly cold, then take off all the fat, and scrape off the dregs that adhere to the jelly. Put the jelly in a preserving kettle, set it on a slow fire—when it melts, take it from the fire, and mix with it half a pint of white wine, the juice and grated rind of a couple of fresh lemons, and a stick of cinnamon or mace. Wash and wipe dry six eggs—take the whites of them, and beat them to a froth—stir them into the jelly when it is cool—bruise the shells, and mix them with the jelly, then set it on a few coals. Sweeten it, when hot, to the taste—white sugar is the best, but brown answers very well. Let the whole boil slowly fifteen minutes, without stirring it—suspend a flannel bag on a nail, and let the jelly drain through it, into a deep dish or pitcher. If it is not clear the first time, let it pass through the bag till it becomes so. The bag should not be squeezed, otherwise the jelly will not look clear. When transparent, turn it into glasses, and set the glasses, if the weather is hot, into cold water, and keep them in a cool place. This kind of jelly will keep but a few days, in warm weather. A knuckle of veal, and sheep's feet, make a nice jelly, prepared in the same manner as calf's feet.

335. *Hartshorn Jelly.*

Boil four ounces of hartshorn shavings in a couple of quarts of water, till it becomes a thick jelly—then strain and put to it the juice and rind of a couple of lemons, a wine glass of white wine, and a stick of cinnamon. Wash four fresh eggs, wipe them dry, separate the whites from the yelks, beat the whites to a froth, bruise the shells, and mix them with the hartshorn—set the whole on a moderate fire—sweeten it to the taste when hot. Boil it till it becomes quite thick, then let it drain through a jelly-bag till clear.

336. *Coffee.*

Old Java and Mocha coffee are the best kinds. Coffee should be put in an iron pot, and dried over a moderate fire for several hours, before it is roasted. It should be put at such a distance from the fire, as to be in no danger of burning. When it has dried three or four hours, set the pot on a hot bed of coals, and stir it constantly, until sufficiently roasted, which is ascertained by biting one of the lightest colored kernels—if it is brittle, the whole is done. Turn it out of the pot immediately, into a box—cover it tight, to keep in the steam. A coffee-roaster is better than a pot to roast coffee in, as it preserves the fine aromatic flavor of the coffee, which in a great measure escapes with the steam of the coffee, when roasted in an open pot. To make good common coffee, allow a table-spoonful of it, when ground, to each pint of water. Turn on the water boiling hot, and boil the coffee in a tin pot, from twenty to twenty-five minutes—if boiled longer, it will not taste fresh and lively. Let it stand, after being taken from the fire, four or five minutes to settle, then turn it off carefully from the grounds, into a coffee-pot or urn. When the coffee is put on the fire to boil, a piece of fish-skin or isinglass, of the size of a nine-pence, should be put in, or else the white and shell of half an egg, to a couple of quarts of coffee. Many persons dislike to clear coffee with fish-skin, thinking that it imparts an unpleasant taste to coffee, but it will not, if properly prepared. The skin should be taken from mild codfish, that has not been soaked, as the skin loses its clearing properties by soaking. Rinse it in cold water, and dry it perfectly. When dried, cut it into pieces of the size of a nine-pence. If torn off, as it is wanted for use, too much is apt to be put in at once, and give the coffee a bad taste. A piece of the size of a twelve and a half cent piece, is sufficient to settle a couple of quarts of water. French coffee is made in a German filter, the water is turned on boiling hot, and one-third more coffee is necessary than when boiled in the common way. Where cream cannot be procured for coffee, the coffee will be much richer to boil it with a less proportion of water than the above rule, and weaken it with boiling hot milk, when served out in cups.

337. *Tea.*

Scald the tea-pot, and if the tea is a strong kind, a tea-spoonful for a pint of water is sufficient—if it is a weak kind, more will be required. Pour on just enough boiling water to cover the tea, and let it steep. Green tea should not steep more than five or six minutes before drinking—if steeped longer, it will not be lively. Black tea requires steeping ten or twelve minutes to extract the strength.

338. *Chocolate.*

Scrape the chocolate off fine, mix it smooth with water—if liked very rich, make the chocolate entirely of milk—if not, use half water. Boil water and milk together, then stir in the chocolate, previously mixed with water—stir it till it boils, then sweeten it to your taste, and take it up. If liked rich, grate in a little nutmeg. A table-spoonful of chocolate to a pint of water or milk, is about the right proportion.

339. *Hop Beer.*

Put to six ounces of hops five quarts of water, and boil them three hours—then strain off the liquor, and put to the hops four quarts more of water, a tea-cup full of ginger, and boil the hops three hours longer. Strain and mix it with the rest of the liquor, and stir in a couple of quarts of molasses. Take about half a pound of bread, and brown it very slowly—when very brown and dry, put it in the liquor, to enrich the beer. Rusked bread is the best for this purpose, but a loaf of bread cut in slices, and toasted till brittle, will do very well. When rusked bread is used, pound it fine, and brown it in a pot, as you would coffee, stirring it constantly. When the hop liquor cools, so as to be just lukewarm, add a pint of new yeast, that has no salt in it. Keep the beer covered in a temperate situation, till it has ceased fermenting, which is ascertained by the subsiding of the froth—turn it off carefully into a beer keg, or bottles. The beer should not be corked very tight, or it will burst the bottles. It should be kept in a cool place.

340. *Beer of Essential Oils.*

Mix a couple of quarts of boiling water with a pint and a half of molasses. Stir in five quarts of cold water, then add ten drops of the oil of sassafras, ten of spruce, fifteen of winter-green, and a tea-spoonful of essence of ginger. When just lukewarm, put in half a pint of fresh lively yeast. When fermented, bottle and cork it, and keep it in a cool place. It will be fit to drink in the course of two or three days.

341. *Spring Beer.*

Take a small bunch of all, or part of the following: Sweet fern, sarsaparilla, winter-green, sassafras, prince's pine, and spice wood. Boil them with two or three ounces of hops to three or four gallons of water, and two or three raw potatoes, pared and cut in slices. The strength of the roots and hops is obtained more thoroughly by boiling them in two waters—for, when the liquor is strongly saturated with the hops, it will rather bind up the roots than extract their juices. The roots should be boiled five or six hours —the liquor should then be strained, and a quart of molasses put to three gallons of the beer. If you wish to have the beer very rich, brown half a pound of bread, and put it into the liquor. If the liquor is too thick, dilute it with cold water. When just lukewarm, put in a pint of fresh lively yeast, that has no salt in it. The salt has a tendency to keep it from fermenting. Keep it in a temperate situation, covered over, but not so tight as to exclude the air entirely, or it will not work. When fermented, keep it in a tight keg, or bottle and cork it up.

342. *Ginger Beer.*

Boil gently, in a gallon of water, three table-spoonsful of cream of tartar, three of ginger, and a lemon cut in slices. When it has boiled half an hour, take it from the fire, strain and sweeten it to your taste—white sugar is the best, but brown sugar or molasses answers very well. Put to it, when lukewarm, half a pint of fresh yeast. Turn it off carefully, when fermented, bottle it, and keep it in a cool place. It will be fit to drink in the course of seven or eight days.

343. *Instantaneous Beer.*

Put to a pint and a half of water four tea-spoonsful of ginger, a table-spoonful of lemon-juice—sweeten it to the taste with syrup or white sugar, and turn it into a junk bottle. Have ready a cork to fit the bottle, a string of wire to tie it down, and a mallet to drive in the cork. Then put into the bottle a heaping tea-spoonful of the super-carbonate of soda, cork it immediately, tie it down, then shake the whole up well, cut the string, and the cork will fly out. Turn it out, and drink immediately.

344. *Mixed Wine.*

Take equal parts of ripe currants, grapes, raspberries, and English cherries. Bruise them, then mix cold water with them, in the proportion of four pounds of fruit to a gallon of water. Let the whole remain half a day. Stir the whole up well, then strain it—to each gallon of it put three pounds of sugar. Keep it in a temperate situation, where it will ferment slowly, three or four days—stir it up frequently. When fermented, add a ninth part of brandy to it, and stop it up tight—when it becomes clear, bottle it. In the course of a year it will be fit to drink.

345. *Currant Wine.*

Strain the currants, which should be perfectly ripe. To each quart of juice put a couple of quarts of water, and three pounds of sugar—stir the whole well together, and let it stand twenty-four hours, without stirring—then skim and set it in a cool place, where it will ferment slowly. Let it remain three or four days—if, at the end of that time, it has ceased fermenting, add one quart of French brandy to every fifteen gallons of the liquor, and close up the barrel tight. When it becomes clear, it is fit to bottle. This will be good in the course of six months, but it is much improved by being kept several years.

346. *Grape Wine.*

Bruise the grapes, which should be perfectly ripe. To each gallon of grapes put a gallon of water, and let the whole remain a week, without being stirred. At the end of that time, draw off the liquor carefully, and put to each gallon three pounds of lump sugar. Let it ferment in a temperate situation—when fermented, stop it up tight. In the course of six months it will be fit to bottle.

347. *To mull Wine.*

To a pint of water put a tea-spoonful of powdered cloves and cinnamon. Set it where it will boil—then separate the whites and yelks of three eggs, and beat the yelks with a large spoonful of powdered white sugar. As soon as the water boils, turn it on to the yelks and sugar—add a pint of wine, and turn the beaten whites of the eggs over the whole.

348. *Quince Cordial.*

Take ripe nice quinces, wipe off the fur, and grate them. Express the juices of the quince pulp through a strong cloth, and to each quart of it put two-thirds of a quart of French brandy, a pound and a half of white sugar, a hundred bitter almonds, or peach meats, a dozen cloves. Put it in a stone pot, cover it tight, and keep it a week in a warm place, then skim and bottle it, and let it remain a year before using it.

349. *Peach Cordial.*

Take ripe juicy peaches—wash and wipe them, to get off the down—gash them to the stone. Put to each peck of peaches a gallon of French brandy, and cover them up tight. Let the whole remain a couple of months, then drain the brandy free from the peaches—add sufficient cold water to render it of the strength of good white wine, and to every three gallons of it put four pounds of sugar. Stir it up well—let it remain a couple of days, stirring it up well each day, then turn it into a wine cask, and close it tight.

350. *Smallage Cordial.*

Take young sprouts of smallage—wash and drain them till perfectly dry. Cut them in small pieces, put them in a bottle, with seeded raisins, having an alternate layer of each. When the bottle is two-thirds full of the smallage, turn in French brandy, till the bottle is full. Let it remain three or four days, to have the smallage absorb the brandy—then put in as much more brandy as the bottle will hold. It will be fit for use in the course of eight or ten days. This is an excellent family medicine.

351. *Currant Shrub.*

To a pint of strained currant juice, put a pound of sugar. Boil the sugar and juice gently together, eight or ten minutes, then set it where it will cool. Add, when lukewarm, a wine glass of French brandy to every pint of syrup—bottle and cork it tight—keep it in a cool place.

352. *Raspberry Shrub.*

To three quarts of fresh, ripe raspberries, put one of good vinegar. Let it remain a day—then strain it, and put to each pint a pound of white sugar. Boil the whole together for half an hour, skim it clear. When cool, add a wine glass of French brandy to each pint of the shrub. A couple of table-spoonsful of this, mixed with a tumbler two-thirds full of water, is a wholesome and refreshing drink in fevers.

353. *Lemon Shrub.*

Procure nice fresh lemons—pare the rind off thin, then squeeze out the juice of the lemons, and strain it. To a pint of the juice put a pound of white sugar, broken into small pieces. Measure out for each pint of the syrup three table-spoonsful of French brandy, and soak the rind of the lemons in it. Let the whole remain a day, stirring up the lemon-juice and sugar frequently. The next day turn off the syrup, and mix it with the brandy and lemon rinds—put the whole in clean bottles, cork and seal them tight, and keep them in dry sand, in a cool place.

354. *Sherbet.*

Boil in three pints of water six or eight green stalks of rhubarb, a quarter of a pound of figs or raisins. When the whole has boiled between twenty-five and thirty minutes, strain it, and mix it with a tea-spoonful of rosewater, and lemon or orange syrup to the taste. Let it get cold before drinking it.

355. *Noyeau.*

To three pints of French brandy, put four ounces of bitter almonds, or peach meats, and a couple of ounces of sweet almonds—they should be bruised before they are mixed with the brandy. Add half an ounce each of powdered cinnamon and mace, a quarter of an ounce of cloves. Let the whole remain a fortnight, shaking it up well each day, then drain off the brandy into another bottle, and put to the almonds a quart of water. Let it stand three days, then turn back the brandy, and put in a pound and a half of white sugar. Let the whole remain a week, stirring it up frequently, then strain the liquor off, free from the dregs, into bottles for use.

356. *Mead.*

Put to a pound of honey three pints of warm water—stir it up well, and let it remain till the honey is held in complete solution—then turn it into a cask, leaving the bung out. Let it ferment in a temperate situation—bottle it as soon as fermented, cork it up very tight.

357. *Essence of Lemon.*

Turn gradually on to a drachm of the best oil of lemons a couple of ounces of strong rectified spirit. The best method of obtaining the essence of the lemon peel, is to rub all the yellow part of the peel off, with lumps of white sugar, and scrape off the surface of the sugar into a preserving pot, as fast as it becomes saturated with the oil of the lemon. The sugar should be pressed down tight, and covered very close. A little of this sugar gives a fine flavor to puddings, cakes, and pies. This mode of preserving the essence of the lemon is superior to the one in which spirit is used, as the fine aromatic flavor of the peel is procured without any alloy.

358. *Essence of Ginger.*

Take three ounces of fresh ginger—grate and put it into a quart of French brandy, together with the rind of a fresh lemon—none of the white part of the peel should be put in. Shake the whole up well every day, for eight or ten days—at the end of that time, it will be fit for use. A little of this, mixed with water, or put on a lump of sugar, answers all the purposes of ginger tea, and is much more palatable. It is also nice to flavor many kinds of sweetmeats.

359. *Spice Brandy.*

Put into a jar French brandy, and rose or peach leaves, in the proportion of a quart of the former to half a pint of the latter. Let them steep together, till the strength is obtained from the leaves—then turn off the brandy, squeeze the leaves dry, throw them away, and put fresh leaves to the brandy. Continue to go through the above process until the brandy is strongly impregnated with the leaves—then turn the brandy off clear, and bottle it—keep it corked tight. Lemon or orange peel, and peach meats, steeped in a bottle of brandy, give it a fine flavor. It takes the rind of three or four lemons, or a quarter of a pound of peach meats, to flavor a pint of brandy. When all the brandy is used, put in more, with a few fresh rinds. Spice brandy is very nice to season cakes, puddings, and mince pies.

360. *Rosewater.*

Gather fragrant, full-blown roses, on a dry day—pick off the leaves, and to each peck of them put a quart of water. Put the whole in a cold still, and set the still on a moderate fire—the slower they are distilled, the better will be the rosewater. Bottle the water as soon as distilled.

361. *To extract the Essential Oil of Flowers.*

Procure a quantity of fresh, fragrant leaves—both the stalk and the flower leaves will answer. Cord very thin layers of cotton, and dip them into fine Florence oil—put alternate layers of the cotton and leaves in a glass jar, or large tumbler. Sprinkle a very small quantity of fine salt on each layer of the flowers, cover the jar up tight, and place it in a south window, exposed to the heat of the sun. In the course of a fortnight a fragrant oil may be squeezed out of the cotton. Rose leaves, mignonette, and sweet-scented clover, make fine perfumes, managed in this way.

362. *Perfume Bags.*

Rose and sweet-scented clover leaves, dried in the shade, then mixed with powdered cloves, cinnamon, mace, and pressed in small bags, are very nice to keep in chests of linen, or drawers of clothes, to perfume them.

363. *Cologne Water.*

Turn a quart of alcohol gradually on to the following oils: a couple of drachms of the oil of rosemary, two of the oil of lemon, or orange-flower water, one drachm of lavender, ten drops of oil of cinnamon, ten of cloves, and a tea-spoonful of rosewater. Keep the whole stopped tight in a bottle—shake it up well. It will do to use as soon as made, but it is much improved by age.

364. *Lavender Water.*

Turn a pint of alcohol slowly on to an ounce and a half of the oil of lavender, two drachms of ambergris. Keep the lavender water in a tight-corked bottle—it should be shook up well when first put in.

365. *Aromatic Vinegar.*

Mix with a table-spoonful of vinegar enough powdered chalk to destroy the acidity. Let it settle—then turn off the vinegar from the chalk carefully, and dry it perfectly. Whenever you wish to purify an infected room, put in a few drops of sulphuric acid—the fumes arising from it will purify a room where there has been any infectious disorder. Care is necessary in using it, not to inhale the fumes, or to get any of the acid on your garments, as it will corrode whatever it touches.

366. *Barley Water.*

Boil a couple of ounces of barley, in two quarts of water, till soft—pearl barley is the best, but the common barley answers very well. When soft, strain and mix it with a little currant jelly, to give it a pleasant, acid taste. If the jelly is not liked, turn it, when boiled soft, on to a couple of ounces of figs or raisins, and boil it again, till reduced to one quart, then strain it for use.

367. *Rice Gruel.*

Put a large spoonful of unground rice into six gills of boiling water, with a stick of cinnamon or mace. Strain it when boiled soft, and add half a pint of new milk—put in a tea-spoonful of salt, and boil it a few minutes longer. If you wish to make the gruel of rice flour, mix a table-spoonful of it, smoothly, with three of cold water, and stir it into a quart of boiling water. Let it boil, five or six minutes, stirring it constantly. Season it with salt, a little butter, and add, if you like, nutmeg and white sugar to your taste.

368. *Water Gruel.*

Mix a couple of table-spoonsful of Indian meal with one of wheat flour, and sufficient cold water to make a thick batter. If the gruel is liked thick, stir it into a pint of boiling water—if liked thin, more water will be necessary. Season the gruel with salt, and let it boil six or eight minutes, stirring it frequently—then take it from the fire, put in a piece of butter, of the size of a walnut, and pepper to the taste. Turn it on toasted bread, cut in small pieces.

369. *Caudle.*

Make rice or water gruel, as above—then strain it, and add half a wine glass of ale, wine, or brandy. Sweeten it with loaf sugar, and grate in a little nutmeg.

370. *Arrow Root Custards.*

Boil a pint of milk, and stir into it, while boiling, a table-spoonful of arrow root, mixed smooth, with a little cold milk. Stir it in well, and let the whole boil three or four minutes—take it from the fire to cool—when so, stir in a couple of beaten eggs, sweeten it to the taste, and grate in a small piece of nutmeg. Set the whole where it will boil, stirring it constantly. As soon as it boils up, take it from the fire, and turn it into custard cups. The arrow root, prepared in the same manner as for the custards, omitting the sugar, spice, and eggs, is excellent food for invalids, and can be eaten when the custards are too rich for the stomach.

371. *Wine Whey.*

Stir into a pint of boiling milk a couple of glasses of wine. Let it boil a minute, then take it from the fire, and let it remain till the curd has settled—then turn off the whey, and sweeten it with white sugar.

372. *Stomachic Tincture.*

Bruise a couple of ounces of Peruvian bark, one of bitter dried orange peel. Steep them in a pint of proof spirit a fortnight, shaking up the bottle that contains it once or twice every day. Let it remain untouched for a couple of days, then decant the bitter into another bottle. A tea-spoonful of this, in a wine glass of water, is a fine tonic.

373. *Thoroughwort Bitters.*

Make a strong tea of the thoroughwort—strain it, and when cool, put to a couple of quarts of it half a pint of French brandy, the peel of two or three fresh oranges, cut into small bits, and half a dozen bunches of fennel, or smallage seed. The seed and orange peel should be crowded into a bottle, then the tea and brandy turned in. The bottle should be corked tight. The bitters will keep good almost any length of time, and is an excellent remedy for bilious complaints, and can often be taken when the thoroughwort tea will not sit on the stomach. A wine glass of these bitters to a tumbler of water is about the right proportion. It should have a little sugar added to it before drinking it.

374. *Cough Tea.*

Make a strong tea of everlasting—strain, and put to a quart of it two ounces of figs or raisins, two of liquorice, cut in bits. Boil them in the tea for twenty minutes, then take the tea from the fire, and add to it the juice of a lemon. This is an excellent remedy for a tight cough—it should be drank freely, being perfectly innocent. It is the most effectual when hot.

375. *Beef Tea.*

Broil a pound of fresh lean beef ten minutes—then cut it into small bits, turn a pint of boiling water on it, and let it steep in a warm place half an hour—then strain it, and season the tea with salt and pepper to the taste. This is a quick way of making the tea, but it is not so good, when the stomach will bear but a little liquid on it, as the following method: Cut the beef into small bits, which should be perfectly free from fat—fill a junk bottle with them, cork it up tight, and immerse it in a kettle of lukewarm water, and boil it four or five hours. This way is superior to the first, on account of obtaining the juices of the meat, unalloyed with water, a table-spoonful of it being as nourishing as a tea-cup full of the other.

376. *Moss Jelly.*

Steep Carragua, or Irish moss, in cold water a few minutes, to extract the bitter taste—then drain off the water, and to half an ounce of moss put a quart of fresh water, and a stick of cinnamon. Boil it till it becomes a thick jelly, then strain it, and season it to the taste with white wine and white sugar. This is very nourishing, and recommended highly for consumptive complaints.

377. *Sago Jelly.*

Rinse four ounces of sago thoroughly, then soak it in cold water half an hour—turn off the water, and put to it a pint and a half of fresh cold water. Let it soak in it half an hour, then set it where it will boil slowly, stirring it constantly—boil with it a stick of cinnamon. When of a thick consistency, add a glass of wine, and white sugar to the taste. Let it boil five minutes, then turn it into cups.

378. *Tapioca Jelly.*

Take four table-spoonsful of tapioca—rinse it thoroughly, then soak it five hours, in cold water enough to cover it. Set a pint of cold water on the fire—when it boils, mash and stir up the tapioca that is in water, and mix it with the boiling water. Let the whole simmer gently, with a stick of cinnamon or mace. When thick and clear, mix a couple of table-spoonsful of white sugar, with half a table-spoonful of lemon-juice, and half a glass of white wine—stir it into the jelly—if not sweet enough, add more sugar, and turn the jelly into cups.

MISCELLANEOUS RECEIPTS RELATIVE TO HOUSEWIFERY.

379. *To renew Old Bread and Cake.*

Fill a bread steamer about half full of water, and lay the dry bread on it, and set it on the fire, where it will steam the bread from half to three-quarters of an hour; then wrap the bread in a towel, and let it remain till dry. In this way, bread that is old and dry may be made moist and good. Where a steamer cannot be procured, soak the bread in cold water till it has absorbed sufficient water to be moist inside—then put it in a bake pan, without any cover, and heat it very hot. If broken pieces of bread are put in the oven, five or six hours after baking, and rusked, they will keep good a long time. Sour heavy bread, treated in this manner, will make very decent cakes and puddings, provided there is enough saleratus used in making them to correct the acidity of the bread. Rich cake, that has wine or brandy in it, will remain good in cold weather several months, if it is kept in a cool, dry place. The day in which it is to be eaten, put it in a cake pan, and set it in a bake pan that has half a pint of water in it—set on the bake-pan cover, and let the cake bake till it is heated very hot. Let it get cold before cutting it.

380. *To preserve Cheese from Insects.*

Cover the cheese, while whole, with a paste made of wheat flour; then wrap a cloth round it, and cover it with the paste. Keep the cheese in a cool, dry place. Cheese that has skippers in it, if kept till cold weather, will be freed from them.

381. *To pot Cheese.*

Cheese that has begun to mould, can be kept from becoming any more so, by being treated in the following manner: Cut off the mouldy part, and if the cheese is dry, grate it—if not, pound it fine in a mortar, together with the crust. To each pound of it, when fine, put a table-spoonful of brandy—mix it in well with the cheese, then press it down tight, in a clean stone pot, and lay a paper wet in brandy on the top of it. Cover the pot up tight, and keep it in a cool, dry place. This is also a good way to treat dry pieces of cheese. Potted cheese is best when a year old. It will keep several years, without any danger of its breeding insects.

382. *To pot Butter for winter use.*

Mix a large spoonful of salt, a table-spoonful of powdered white-sugar, and one of saltpetre. Work this quantity into six pounds of fresh-made butter. Put the butter into a stone pot, that is thoroughly cleansed. When you have finished putting down your butter, cover it with a layer of salt, and let it remain covered until cold weather.

383. *To make Salt Butter Fresh.*

When butter has too much salt in it, put to each pound of it a quart of fresh milk, and churn it an hour; then treat it like fresh butter, working in the usual quantity of salt. A little white sugar worked in, improves it. This is said to be equal to fresh butter. Salt may be taken out of a small quantity of fresh butter, by working it over, in clear fresh water, changing the water a number of times.

384. *To extract Rancidity from Butter.*

Take a small quantity, that is wanted for immediate use. For a pound of the butter, dissolve a couple of tea-spoonsful of saleratus in a quart of boiling water, put in the butter, mix it well with the saleratus water, and let it remain till cold, then take it off carefully, and work a tea-spoonful of salt into it. Butter treated in this manner answers very well to use in cooking.

385. *To preserve Cream for Sea Voyages.*

Take rich, fresh cream, and mix it with half of its weight of white powdered sugar. When well mixed in, put it in bottles, and cork them tight. When used for tea or coffee, it will make them sufficiently sweet without any additional sugar.

386. *Substitute for Cream in Coffee.*

Beat the white of an egg to a froth—put to it a small lump of butter, and turn the coffee to it gradually, so that it may not curdle. It is difficult to distinguish the taste from fresh cream.

387. *To keep Eggs several months.*

It is a good plan to buy eggs for family use when cheap, and preserve them in the following manner: Mix half a pint of unslaked lime with the same quantity of salt, a couple of gallons of water. The water should be turned on boiling hot. When cold, put in the eggs, which should be perfectly fresh, and care should be taken not to crack any of them—if cracked, they will spoil directly. The eggs should be entirely covered with the lime-water, and kept in a stone pot, and the pot set in a cool place. If the above directions are strictly attended to, the eggs will keep good five months. The lime-water should not be so strong as to eat the shell, and all the eggs should be perfectly fresh when put in, as one bad one will spoil the whole.

388. *To melt Fat for Shortening.*

The fat of all kinds of meat, excepting that of ham and mutton, makes good shortening. Roast meat drippings, and the liquor in which meat is boiled, should stand until cold, to have the fat congeal, so that it can be taken off easily. When taken up, scrape off the sediment which adheres to the under side of the fat, cut the fat into small pieces, together with any scraps of fat from broiled meat that you may happen to have. Melt the fat slowly, then strain it, and let it remain till cold. When formed into a hard cake, take it up—if any sediment adheres to the under side, scrape it off. Melt the fat again—when partly cooled, sprinkle in salt, in the proportion of a tea-spoonful to a pound of the shortening. The dregs of the fat are good for soap grease. This shortening answers all the various purposes of lard very well, excepting in the hottest weather. The fat of cooked meat should not be suffered to remain more than a week in winter, and three days in summer, without being melted. Ham fat, if boiled in fresh water, and then clarified, answers very well to fry in. Mutton fat, if melted into hard cakes, will fetch a good price at the tallow-chandler's. The leaves, and thin pieces of pork, should be used for lard. Cut them in small bits, and melt them slowly; then strain them through a cullender, with a thick cloth laid in it. As soon as the fat cools and thickens, sprinkle in salt, in the proportion of a tea-cup full to twenty weight of the lard. Stir it in well, then set the pot that contains it in a cool place. Some people have an idea that the pork scraps must be on the fire until they become brown, in order to have the lard kept sweet the year round, but it is not necessary, if salt is mixed with it.

389. *To keep Vegetables through the Winter.*

Succulent vegetables are preserved best in a cool, shady place, that is damp. Turnips, Irish potatoes, and similar vegetables, should be protected from the air and frost by being buried up in sand, and in very severe cold weather covered over with a linen cloth. It is said that the dust of charcoal, sprinkled over potatoes, will keep them from sprouting. I have also heard it said, that Carolina potatoes may be kept a number of months, if treated in the following manner: Take those that are large, and perfectly free from decay—pack them in boxes of dry sand, and set the boxes in a place exposed to the influence of smoke, and inaccessible to frost.

390. *To preserve Herbs.*

All kinds of herbs should be gathered on a dry day, just before, or while in blossom. Tie them in bundles, and suspend them in a dry, airy place, with the blossoms downwards. When perfectly dry, wrap the medicinal ones in paper and keep them from the air. Pick off the leaves of those which are to be used in cooking, pound and sift them fine, and keep the powder in bottles, corked up tight.

391. *To preserve various kinds of Fruit through the Winter.*

Apples can be kept till June, by taking only those that are hard and sound, wiping them dry, then packing them in tight barrels, with a layer of bran to each layer of apples. Envelope the barrel in a linen cloth, to protect it from frost, and keep it in a cool place, but not so cold as to freeze the apples. It is said that mortar, laid over the top of a barrel of apples, is a good thing to preserve them, as it draws the air from them, which is the principal cause of their decaying. Care should be taken not to have it come in contact with the apples. To preserve oranges and lemons several months, take those that are perfectly fresh, and wrap each one in soft paper; put them in glass jars, or a very tight box, with white sand, that has been previously dried in an oven a few hours, after it has been baked in. The sand should be strewed thick over each one of the oranges, as they are laid in the jar, and the whole covered with a thick layer of it. Close the jar up tight, and keep it in a cool dry place, but not so cool as to freeze the fruit. To preserve grapes, gather them on a dry day, when they are not quite dead ripe, and pick those that are not fair off from the stems. Lay the bunches of grapes in a glass jar, and sprinkle around each of them a thick layer of dry bran, so that they will not touch each other. Have a thick layer of bran on the top, and cork and seal the jar very tight, so that the air may be entirely excluded. Whenever they are to be eaten, restore them to their freshness by cutting off a small piece from the end of the stalks, and immerse the stalks of each bunch in sweet wine for a few minutes. The stalks will imbibe the wine, and make the grapes fresh and juicy. Various kinds of fruit, taken when green, such as grapes, gooseberries, currants, and plums, can be kept through the winter, by being treated in the following manner: Fill junk bottles with them, and set them in an oven six or seven hours, after having baked in it. Let them remain till they begin to shrink, then take the fruit from one bottle to fill the others quite full. Cork and seal up the bottles. Whenever you wish to make pies of them, put the quantity you wish to use into a tin pan, turn on boiling water sufficient to cover them, and stew them in it till soft, then sweeten, and make them into pies. Ripe blackberries and whortleberries, to be kept long, should be dried perfectly in the sun, then tied up in bags that are thick enough to exclude the air. When used for pies, treat them in the same manner as the green fruit. Ripe currants, dried on the stalks, then picked off, and put in bags, will keep nice for pies during the winter. They also make a fine tea for persons that have a fever, particularly the hectic fever—it is also an excellent thing to counteract the effects of opium.

392. *To keep Pickles and Sweetmeats.*

Pickles should be kept in unglazed earthen jars, or wooden kegs. Sweetmeats keep best in glass jars; unglazed stone pots answer very well for common fruit. A paper wet in brandy, or proof spirit, and laid on the preserved fruit, tends to keep it from fermenting. Both pickles and sweetmeats should be watched, to see that they do not ferment, particularly when the weather is warm. Whenever they ferment, turn off the vinegar or syrup, scald and turn it back while hot. When pickles grow soft, it is owing to the vinegar being too weak. To strengthen it, heat it scalding hot, turn it back on the pickles, and when lukewarm, put in a little alum, and a brown paper, wet in molasses. If it does not grow sharp in the course of three weeks it is past recovery, and should be thrown away, and fresh vinegar turned on, scalding hot, to the pickles.

393. *Cautions relative to the use of Brass and Copper Cooking Utensils.*

Cleanliness has been aptly styled the cardinal virtue of cooks. Food is more healthy, as well as palatable, cooked in a cleanly manner. Many lives have been lost in consequence of carelessness in using brass, copper, and glazed earthen cooking utensils. The two first should be thoroughly cleansed with salt and hot vinegar before cooking in them, and no oily or acid substance, after being cooked, should be allowed to cool or remain in any of them.

394. *Durable Ink for Marking Linen.*

Dissolve a couple of drachms of lunar caustic, and half an ounce of gum arabic, in a gill of rain water. Dip whatever is to be marked in strong pearl-ash water. When perfectly dry, iron it very smooth; the pearl-ash water turns it a dark color, but washing will efface it. After marking the linen, put it near a fire, or in the sun, to dry. Red ink, for marking linen, is made by mixing and reducing to a fine powder half an ounce of vermilion, a drachm of the salt of steel, and linseed oil to render it of the consistency of black durable ink.

395. *Black Ball.*

Melt together, moderately, ten ounces of Bayberry tallow, five ounces of bees' wax, one ounce of mutton tallow. When melted, add lamp or ivory black to give it a good black color. Stir the whole well together, and add, when taken from the fire, half a glass of rum.

396. *Liquid Blacking.*

Mix a quarter of a pound of ivory black, six gills of vinegar, a tablespoonful of sweet oil, two large spoonsful of molasses. Stir the whole well together, and it will then be fit for use.

397. *Cement for the Mouths of Corked Bottles.*

Melt together a quarter of a pound of sealing-wax, the same quantity of rosin, a couple of ounces of bees' wax. When it froths, stir it with a tallow candle. As soon as it melts, dip the mouths of the corked bottles into it. This is an excellent thing to exclude the air from such things as are injured by being exposed to it.

398. *Cement for broken China, Glass, and Earthenware.*

Rub the edge of the china or glass with the beaten white of an egg. Tie very finely powdered quick lime in a muslin bag, and sift it thick over the edges of the dishes that have been previously rubbed with the egg. Match and bind the pieces together, and let it remain bound several weeks. This is good cement for every kind of crockery but thick heavy glass and coarse earthenware; the former cannot be cemented with any thing; for the latter, white paint will answer. Paint and match the broken edges, bind them tight together, and let them remain until the paint becomes dry and hard. Milk is a good cement for crockery—the pieces should be matched, and bound together tight, then put in cold milk, and the milk set where it will boil for half an hour; then take it from the fire, and let the crockery remain till the milk is cold. Let the crockery remain bound for several weeks. The Chinese method of mending broken china, is to grind flint glass, on a painter's stone, till it is reduced to an impalpable powder: then beat it with the white of an egg, to a froth, and lay it on the edge of the broken pieces, match and bind them together firmly, and let them remain several weeks. It is said that no art will then be able to break it in the same place.

399. *Japanese Cement, or Rice Glue.*

Mix rice flour with cold water, to a smooth paste, and boil it gently. It answers all the purposes of wheat flour paste, while it is far superior in point of transparency and smoothness. This composition, made with so small a proportion of water as to have it of the consistence of plastic clay, may be used to form models, busts, basso-relievos, and similar articles. When made of it, they are susceptible of a very high polish. Poland starch is a nice cement for pasting layers of paper together, or any fancy articles.

400. *Cement for Alabaster.*

Take of white bees' wax one pound, of rosin a pound, and three quarters of alabaster. Melt the wax and rosin, then strew the alabaster over it lightly, (which should be previously reduced to a fine powder.) Stir the whole well together, then knead the mass in water, in order to incorporate the alabaster thoroughly with the rosin and wax. The alabaster, when mended, should be perfectly dry, and heated. The cement, when applied, should also be heated. Join the broken pieces, bind them, and let them remain a week. This composition, when properly managed, forms an extremely strong cement.

401. *To clean Alabaster, or any other kinds of Marble.*

Pound pumice stone to a fine powder, and mix it with verjuice. Let it remain several hours, then dip in a perfectly clean sponge, and rub the marble with it till clean. Rinse it off with clear fresh water, and rub it dry with a clean linen cloth.

402. *Cement for Iron-ware.*

Beat the whites of eggs to a froth, then stir into them enough quicklime to make a consistent paste, then add iron file dust, to make a thick paste. The quicklime should be reduced to a fine powder before mixing it with the eggs. Fill the cracks in iron-ware with this cement, and let them remain several weeks before using them.

403. *To loosen the Stopples of Decanters and Smelling Bottles that are wedged in tight.*

Dip the end of a feather in oil, and rub it round the stopple, close to the mouth of the bottle; then put the bottle about a couple of feet from the fire, having the mouth towards it. The heat will cause the oil to run down between the stopple and mouth of the bottle. When warm, strike the bottle gently on both sides, with any light wooden instrument that you may happen to have. If the stopple cannot be taken out with the hand at the end of this process, repeat it, and you will finally succeed by persevering in it, however firmly it may be wedged in.

404. *Lip Salve.*

Dissolve a small lump of white sugar in a table-spoonful of rosewater, (common water will do, but is not as good.) Mix it with a couple of large spoonsful of sweet oil, a piece of spermaceti, of the size of half a butternut. Simmer the whole well together eight or ten minutes, then turn it into a small box.

405. *Cold Cream.*

Take of the oil of almonds two ounces, of spermaceti half an ounce, and white wax half an ounce. Put them in a close vessel, and set the vessel in a skillet of boiling water. When melted, beat the ingredients with rosewater until cold. Keep it in a tight box, or wide-mouthed bottle, corked up close.

406. *To prevent the formation of a Crust on Tea-Kettles.*

Keep an oyster-shell in your tea-kettle, and it will prevent the formation of a crust on the inside of it, by attracting the stony particles to itself.

407. *To remove Stains from Broadcloth.*

Take an ounce of pipe clay that has been ground fine, and mix it with twelve drops of alcohol, and the same quantity of spirits of turpentine. Whenever you wish to remove any stains from cloth, moisten a little of this mixture with alcohol, and rub it on the spots. Let it remain till dry, then rub it off with a woollen cloth, and the spots will disappear.

408. *To extract Paint from Cotton, Silk, and Woollen Goods.*

Saturate the spot with spirits of turpentine, and let it remain several hours, then rub it between the hands. It will crumble away, without injuring either the color or texture of the article.

409. *To remove Black Stains on Scarlet Woollen Goods.*

Mix tartaric with water, to give it a pleasant acid taste, then saturate the black spots with it, taking care not to have it touch the clean part of the garment. Rinse the spots immediately, in fair water. Weak pearl-ash water is good to remove stains that are produced by acids.

410. *To extract Grease from Silks, Paper, Woollen Goods, and Floors.*

To remove grease spots from goods and paper, grate on them, very thick, French chalk, (common chalk will answer, but is not as good as the French chalk.) Cover the spots with brown paper, and set on a moderately warm iron, and let it remain till cold. Care must be taken not to have the iron so hot as to scorch or change the color of the cloth. If the grease does not appear to be out on removing the iron, grate on more chalk, heat the iron again, and put it on. Repeat the process till the grease is entirely out. Strong pearl-ash water, mixed with sand, and rubbed on grease spots in floors, is one of the most effective things that can be used to extract the grease.

411. *To extract Stains from White Cotton Goods and Colored Silks.*

Salts of ammonia, mixed with lime, will take out the stains of wine from silk. Spirits of turpentine, alcohol, and clear ammonia, are all good to remove stains on colored silks. Spots of common or durable ink can be removed by saturating them with lemon-juice, and rubbing on salt, then

www.ingramcontent.com/pod-product-compliance
Lightning Source LLC
Chambersburg PA
CBHW081115080526
44587CB00021B/3602